International Students
in First-Year Writing

International Students in First-Year Writing

A Journey Through Socio-Academic Space

MEGAN M. SICZEK

The George Washington University

University of Michigan Press
Ann Arbor

ISBN-13: 978-0-472-03712-4 (paper)
ISBN-13: 978-0-472-12447-3 (ebook)

2021   2020   2019   2018   4   3   2   1

THIS BOOK IS DEDICATED TO Margaret Lucille Hones Siczek, my wonderful grandmother who is nearing her 100th birthday as this manuscript is being finalized. With many celebrations planned, the idea of honoring *experience as lived* is manifest in her path through life from the Great Depression and World War II through her college education, subsequent career, and long and active retirement. She raised a family that grew to include children, grandchildren, great-grandchildren, and even a great-great-grandchild. Through all these stages of history and her own life, she has demonstrated a continuity of self and spirit, embodied in her open-mindedness, deep Catholic faith, sharp intellect, and clever sense of humor. She has been the centerpiece of our family for as long as I remember, and there is no one I treasure more in this world.

—MMS

Acknowledgments

My biggest debt of gratitude is owed to my ten participants, who shared their experiences and interpretations of this remarkable phenomenon. Their bravery and openness was an inspiration, and their voices give power to our understanding of this transnational experience. A special thanks to Brian Casemore, Melinda Knight, and Laura Engel, as well as Joel Gomez and Andy Sonn, for the many ways they supported me and provided feedback on my original study. I'd also like to acknowledge the work of scholars in the field of L2 writing, who have helped me improve my own work as a scholar and as a teacher. I hope this book will find a place among the amazing body of literature produced in our field and that its relevance will cross boundaries into other fields as well. I'm especially grateful for the many contributions my editor Kelly Sippell made to this book. My stopping by the University of Michigan publication booth at a conference was the start of a great collaborative relationship, as well as a new friendship.

I would also like to offer my sincere gratitude to others who supported me throughout this process: To my parents for supporting me in my educational—and indeed in all—endeavors, and for their sense of wonder and pride when I talk about my scholarly work. To my lovely grandmother, Margaret Siczek, to whom this book is dedicated. To Ian Smith, who always makes my home life happy, safe, and stress free. To Guinness, Guillermo, and Olive who were always overjoyed to see me no matter what time I walked in the door. To my friends and family who gave me outlets for talking about this work and encouraged me at every turn, especially Guadalupe Duron, Christiane Connors, Dora Corrado King, Muggs and Jerry Widelski, and Mary Pat and John Young.

Contents

Introduction:
The Forward Arc of Projection

What leads an 18-year-old Chinese woman to pack up her things and fly across the world to study at a U.S. university? She carries with her all she has accumulated over her life and all that has been shaped by generations—if not centuries—of sociocultural history? This journey across cultural spaces is engendered by a particular policy context: the recruitment and enrollment of international students in U.S. institutions of higher education, often driven by global flows as well as an active institutional agenda for internationalization. And where do such students land? Among other places, they land within our institutional curricular frameworks and classrooms. A pilot interview for the research this book is based on captured this young Chinese student's perception at a moment of entry: When registering for a section of the university's required first-year writing course, she felt a sense of connection with one of the sections whose course title implied the "rewriting" of the classic novel *Jane Eyre*. She remembered that she "had much feeling" about the topic because she had read the book *Jane Eyre* as a middle school student in China, and she was "really interested" in what the American teacher would tell her about it. Throughout her life, she had related to the character of Jane Eyre because she viewed herself as an independent woman like Jane and also had a sense of self that shaped her experience within a particular historical period.

This student's hopeful feeling about the course content, however, was tempered by her confusion at the notion of being asked to "rewrite" this classic novel: "Do I need to rewrite the whole book?" she asked herself, "Does this mean the writer is not good?" Then after reading the syllabus on the first day of class, she considered withdrawing and changing to what she thought would be a less challenging section of the course. She found the content of the syllabus to be dense and filled with terms she had never heard before, and she felt that the weighted grade of writing assignments was overwhelming. Her heart became heavy, but she spoke with friends and reflected and, in the end, decided to persist because the class had initially piqued her interest. In early class meetings, she was attentive but quiet, finding that by the time she had formulated her words enough to share something in the class discussion, someone else had already made a similar point. She knew that active participation was a component of the final grade, so she was highly aware of the need to contribute to class activities and discussions, but she found it hard to explain her ideas and worried that others could not understand her spoken English. Though initially she felt she was "not in this class" and was more like an outsider, her confidence grew when an American classmate referenced a comment of hers in a class discussion and when she realized that some of the American students in the class had not even read the book *Jane Eyre* before. How does the rest of her journey unfold?

The central content of this book explores this journey for ten second language (L2) international students, all of whom had migrated transnationally to pursue an undergraduate degree in an urban, private research-intensive university in the United States. Through a series of three interviews during the semester that participants were enrolled in a mainstream first-year writing (FYW) course, the "arc" of their experience was captured over time, starting as they were "projected" forward into this new socio-academic space and culminating with their reflections as they completed this experience.

In other words, I sought to understand the *lived experience* of these participants in a U.S. curricular context, to understand how they constructed and revealed their experiences in this mediated socio-academic space. Because an understanding of this derives

from both a description of the facts of the lived experience—
a phenomenological approach—and an interpretation of its
meaning—a hermeneutic consideration—I applied van Manen's
(1990) action sensitive pedagogic approach to this research. Part
of my pedagogic intent for this study was influenced by my own
role as an educator and my belief that the findings of studies
like this can inform both policy and praxis. Once a description of the lived experience of diverse students illuminates our
understanding of this phenomenon, we can then open up our
own perspectives on the overall trend of internationalization,
as well as our institutional policies and practices. This is based
on the fundamental premise that our consciousness links us
to the world. By intentionally entering into the experience of
others, "our presuppositions are thrown into relief, exposed in
new ways, and made available for revision" (McCaffrey, Raffin-
Bouchal, & Moules, 2012, p. 217).

I have always been broadly interested in the movement of
people across borders and have directed much of my own recent
scholarly work toward the discourses and practices related to
the internationalization of education and the development of
global perspectives and competencies. On a more local level,
in my everyday teaching of L2 writing I am focused on helping international students develop both the knowledge and
skills to manage the expectations of university-level writing in
the United States. I also act as an advocate for the international
student population on campus whenever I can. In my opinion,
the presence of international students—in growing numbers—
on U.S. campuses is often touted as evidence that schools are
globally connected. Yet at the same time, L2 students tend to
be viewed through a deficit perspective by administrators, faculty, and fellow students and may be isolated academically and
socially from the mainstream academic community. We would
all benefit from a deeper and more reflective understanding of
these culturally and linguistically diverse students.

This project originated out of those interests and concerns as
well as a recurring anecdotal experience of mine: Every semester, when L2 students leave my English for Academic Purposes

(EAP) writing class to go on to take the mainstream FYW course that is required of all undergraduate students, I listen to their concerns about which section of the course to choose. Though each of the sections shares the same overall objectives and writing expectations, the thematic content of each instructor's course is different—a policy decision that was intended to enable students to choose a theme that aligned with their intellectual interests. L2 students go to the writing program website and see course options, for example, that link Darwin to U.S. politics, examine the use of African-American speech in public domains, or explore American cultural identity through the lens of Western film. These are innovative and intellectually challenging course themes and potentially powerful platforms for critical thinking, argumentation, and writing at a university level. Yet, as I try to explain to L2 students what the genre of Western film is or its intimate connection to the American identity, I often think: *In addition to the pressures of writing on that level, how will they respond to the content expectations of the class?* particularly when many American students will have a more natural fluency with the thematic content, including its underlying assumptions and knowledge domains. What does it feel like to be a student coming into such a course from the position of a cultural or linguistic outsider, expected to interact with the thematic content, with assignments and activities, and with their American peers and instructor?

The Socio-Academic Space Model

A key contribution of this book is the conceptual model this study engendered. Though existing research explores various aspects of L2 students' experiences—for example, campus acculturation, writing or language development, writing processes, interaction with peers or instructors—this book advocates for the classroom itself to be considered a socio-academic space and a unique site for research. In short, the classroom is a socio-culturally constructed "space," in line with the constructionist theory that learning is a profoundly situated social activity

Figure I.1: The Conceptual Model: Socio-Academic Space

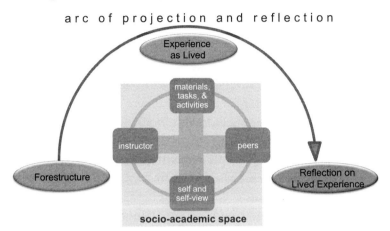

(Watson-Gegeo, 2004; Zuengler & Miller, 2006). Figure I.1 illustrates the way I have envisioned my socio-academic space model.

Though situated in a specific classroom context, that of a theme-based FYW course at a U.S. university, the conceptual model that emerged out of this study has relevance across myriad classroom and institutional contexts. It is socioculturally grounded, drawing on German philosopher Hans-Georg Gadamer's advancement of Heidegger's notion of "thrownness," in which individuals are thrown or projected into new experiences informed by the sociocultural history and the forestructure that shaped their previous understandings. Once projected into a new experience, in this case the socio-academic space of a U.S. college writing class, they engage in mediated activities with others in that setting. Their navigation of the experience—both the details of the experience as "lived" and how they make meaning of the experience—then shapes their future understandings and perspectives.

The content of this book has direct relevance for educators across disciplines, particularly writing program administrators and faculty of writing and writing-intensive courses. It would also be of interest to policymakers and to scholars across fields such as second language writing, applied linguistics, second language acquisition, writing studies, international education, higher education, and curriculum and instruction. Though not necessarily intended for use in a course, this book could be of value for those pursuing graduate coursework in composition/rhetoric, TESOL (Teaching English to Speakers of Other Languages), international education, or even qualitative research studies. Readers will conclude this book with an understanding of the multiple forces that shape global mobility on a higher educational level while deeply engaging with these participants' individual stories as expressed in their own voices. These narrative accounts—thematically analyzed across participants—help readers connect the particular to the universal, a key tool in developing an understanding of a phenomenon. In fact, we can apply Gadamer's "arc of projection and reflection" to readers' interaction with this text: By entering the world of this book, we invite intentional reflection that then informs our future understandings, attitudes, and practices—particularly as they relate to the growing number of culturally and linguistically diverse students in our educational communities.

This book is organized broadly as follows: Chapters 1 through 4 introduce and situate the study and its participants; Chapters 5 through 7 provide vivid description and interpretation of the "arc" of the lived experience at three points in time: the beginning, middle, and end of the semester in which participants were enrolled in the mainstream first-year writing course. Chapters 8 through 10 revisit participant perspectives as they reflect from a distance, present analysis of the key themes and implications of the research, and offer conclusions and recommendations.

1

The Forces That Combine
to Create the Experience

This chapter sets the framework that helps us understand these participants' experiences in a mainstream first-year writing classroom in a U.S. university. The "forces" outlined in this chapter—internationalization of higher education, research on the experiences of international students in U.S. higher education, and their experiences in curricular settings, including first-year writing—inform our understanding by contextualizing their particular experiences more broadly. This, in turn, help us understand this research in ways that go beyond an individual's personal experience. In other words, by building individual experiences into a collective framework, we can enhance our understanding of the broader phenomenon.

The Internationalization of Higher Education

The presence of L2 international students in our classrooms is both a product of and a testament to global interconnectivity. The Organization for Economic Cooperation and Development (OECD) estimated that student mobility at the tertiary level would exceed five million in 2014, with approximately 8 million globally mobile students projected by 2025 (ICEF, 2014). Further, according to the Institute for International Education's (2016) frequently cited *Open Doors* report, more than a million students

1

came from abroad to study in U.S. higher educational institutions in 2015–2016, the highest number on record to date. A driving force behind the internationalization of higher education is the need to respond to the dynamic and diverse conditions of our globally connected world (American Council on Education, 2012; Brustein, 2007; Hunter, White, & Godbey, 2006). As such, higher education institutions have a responsibility to prepare students to inhabit this shared world community and interact in its global marketplace.

Fulfilling such a responsibility requires a shared understanding of what *internationalization* means, which can be complicated by the fact that various stakeholders interpret this priority differently. In fact, though many colleges and universities have accelerated their internationalization activities (Altbach & Knight, 2007; Brustein, 2007; Hayward, 2000; Qiang, 2003), few have a strong or clearly articulated conception of how it can be systematically operationalized on their campuses or even what the term means. Knight (2004) offered a definition that provides a strong foundation for understanding this concept: At an institutional level, she characterized internationalization as "the process of integrating an international, intercultural, or global dimension into the purpose, functions or delivery of post-secondary education" (p. 11). She deliberately emphasized the three dimensions of internationalization to encompass the breadth of this undertaking: *Intercultural* understanding can be a response to diversity within a community; *international* can refer to relationships between countries or cultures; and *global* offers a wider perspective that is inclusive of linkages around the world. She and others have also emphasized that internationalization is an ongoing, dynamic, and integrative process that needs to be responsive to opportunities and sustained across time and space, but that institutions vary in the extent to which internationalization is central to their educational activities (de Wit, 1999; Green, 2003; Knight, 2004; Qiang, 2003). This in part derives from the sheer complexity of the higher education endeavor, including its multiple goals and stakeholders and its diverse institutional arrangements and internal cultures (Bartell, 2003; Childress, 2009; Van der Wende 1999, 2001).

A variety of activities have been associated with internationalization, with target foci that include articulated institutional commitment; administrative structure and staffing; curriculum, co-curriculum, and learning outcomes; faculty policies and practices; student mobility—including study abroad and enrolling international students; and global collaborations and partnerships (American Council on Education, 2012). Many internationalization activities, such as branch campuses and international student recruiting, are cultivated external to U.S. campuses and seem to regard "higher education as a commodity to be sold to growing consumer markets across the world" (Dolby & Rahman, 2008, p. 686). In fact, in today's economy, many colleges and universities are actively capitalizing on the revenue-generating potential of international students and stepping up their marketing and recruitment efforts (Brennan & Dellow, 2013; Stromquist, 2007; Taylor, 2004). It has been estimated that international students and their dependents contributed $32.8 billion dollars to the U.S. economy in the academic year 2015–2016, supporting more than 400,000 jobs (NAFSA, 2016), with a significant proportion of this revenue directly contributed to U.S. higher educational institutions in the form of tuition and fees. A 2013 *Chronicle of Higher Education* survey of 436 private and state universities found that institutions that increased the number of matriculated international students "were more likely to meet enrollment and net-tuition revenue goals," even in tough economic times (Thomason, 2013). Much of the existing research tends to focus on broad trends in global student flows (American Council on Education, 2012; NAFSA, 2016) and rationales and strategies for internationalization (Altbach & Knight, 2007; Brustein, 2007; Qiang, 2003) with less emphasis placed on students' unique backgrounds and motivations and limited discussion of how they traverse spaces, manage risks, and productively interact in global society.

The main content of this book invites us to move beyond statistics and big-picture notions in order to understand the unique experiences of the individuals involved. Considering the lived experience of individuals who migrate transnationally for educational purposes moves us beyond the narrow view of how international students "fit" into the internationalization frameworks that institutions have constructed. These students should not be primarily measured in terms of the extent to which they contribute financial revenues, symbolize the diversity of student populations, or adapt to existing institutional environments. Rather, if institutions are to move toward their stated goal of global learning, then research should value the voices and perspectives of those who have crossed borders to study side by side with domestic students.

International Student Experiences in U.S. Higher Education

Though this book focuses on the international student experience in a particular setting, a mainstream first-year writing (FYW) class in an American university, an understanding of this phenomenon can be shaped by looking at the broader body of recent literature on international student experiences in colleges and universities, which tends to focus on core areas related to adjustment and acculturation:

- *Adjustment:* Adjustment challenges for international students in higher education tend to be different and more significant than those experienced by domestic students; the literature frequently refers to issues of anxiety, stress, social isolation, depression, and homesickness. Acculturation challenges can be mitigated if strong support networks are built and maintained, either through contact with home or with other international or domestic students in the institutional setting, although relationships with domestic students have tended to be more challenging to establish (Andrade, 2006; de Araujo, 2011; Misra, Crist, & Burant, 2003; Smith & Khawaja, 2011).
- *English language proficiency:* Research on the experience of international students in higher education contexts frequently identifies English language proficiency as a mediating factor in students' experiences; in some cases,

lower levels of language proficiency were associated with higher levels of acculturative stress, and perceptions of English language proficiency appeared to have an ongoing effect on students' social and academic experiences in colleges and universities (Andrade, 2006; Chen, 1999; de Araujo, 2011; Mori, 2000; Smith & Khawaja, 2011; Yeh & Inose, 2003).

- *Academic adjustment:* Research indicates that academic adjustment is influenced by English language fluency but also highlights the role expectations play in international students' academic adjustment; in other words, there can be a mismatch between what students expected from the university environment and what they actually experience. Adaptation to this new academic environment can be negatively impacted when students feel pressure to succeed or when they enter classroom settings where the pedagogical approach, level of formality, or expectations for student engagement are significantly different than that of their home culture (Chen, 1999; Mori, 2000; Smith & Khawaja, 2011). Andrade (2006), however, noted that international students may be able to overcome academic challenges more easily than social challenges in the new setting due to their level of motivation, effort, or persistence.
- *Cross-cultural interactions:* Other research notes student perceptions and experiences with discrimination (Lee & Rice, 2007; Smith & Khawaja, 2011; Wadsworth, Hecht & Jung, 2008). Challenges in cross-cultural interaction are also a prevalent theme (Lewthwaite, 1996; Ward & Searle, 1991) in the literature. Surprisingly, there appears to be scant research on the role that interaction with Western cultural content or knowledge plays in shaping international students' socio-academic experiences in U.S. colleges and universities.

In the phenomenological literature on international student experiences, a number of studies also emphasize the

acculturation experience, whether positive or negative, of international students studying in the United States. Several studies have been oriented phenomenologically in order to draw
out essential themes that characterize this experience. Halic,
Greenberg, and Paulus (2009) took a constructivist approach to
their study of eight international graduate students at a large
pubic research university, engaging in an interpretive analysis
of interview transcripts to identify themes that related to language, academic identity, and accessing a new community of
practice. Their findings emphasized the experience of being "in
between," both linguistically and culturally, as well as the constant negotiation of balancing one's self and identity while gaining access to the new academic setting. Being a part of this new
environment sometimes necessitated a selective approach to cultural knowledge and values; for example, participants noted that
they "appropriated only parts of the American culture rather
than being fully engaged" and that they simultaneously reas-
sessed certain aspects of their home culture and "progressively
renounced beliefs that they no longer valued" (p. 85). The phenomenological approach used in their study offered a first-hand
account of students' perceptions and responses, and though
much of the discussion centered around identity and positioning within the new culture, language was a notable mediating
factor. Participants' perception of their language skills, and the
influence of this proficiency on their academic experiences, had
a profound impact on their self-esteem.

Singh and Thuraisingam (2007) conducted phenomenological research on 21 international students from seven countries in
an English-medium university in Malaysia. Approaching sociocultural adjustment through Hofstede's 1980 cultural dimensions
framework, the authors identified five emergent themes that they
called "strangeness, expectations and disillusionment; divides
and bonds; perceptions, prejudices and culture; challenges and
achievement; and social supports and neglect." A key implication of this study's findings was that institutions need to orient
themselves to cultural diversity and cross-cultural interactions
within their teaching and learning environments. Hung and

Hyun (2010) employed a more hermeneutic interpretation in their study of seven international graduate students and four faculty members, tracing participants' experiences through a path of acculturation in which they moved from feeling overly aware of their position as speakers of other languages to being less aware of this position as a result of increased language competencies.

These hermeneutic phenomenological studies certainly have value in that they offer us a multidimensional view of students' experiences in their own words. At the same time, a focus on adjustment/acculturation to the dominant culture is limited in many ways. At the core, it seems to assume that a one-way adaptation is preferable or that assimilation is the goal, and thus that cultural difference or diversity is somehow a deficit. In addition, by narrowing our view of international students' experiences to "acculturation," as researchers and practitioners we may create a barrier between ourselves and our diverse students (with implied power designations), oversimplify a highly complex and dynamic experience, and perhaps overlook the construction of the "self" in the context of transnational mobility.

This study aligns with two conceptual pieces that advocate for evolving our research approach toward one that does not measure international students' experience based on how well they fit into our existing institutional frameworks. Kell and Vogl (2008) questioned the conventional acculturation approach as a "totalizing process that does little to capture the individualized and collective experience of many students" (p. 22). The traditional use of manufactured thematic categories tends to have "superficial connections with reality that have the effect of impeding the understanding and complexity of diversity" (p. 23). They suggested exploring the experiences of international students through a more dynamic and organic framework, one that considers the way students traverse spaces, manage risks, and productively interact in global society. Fred Dervin (2011) also argued for a new "liquid" approach in research on intercultural discourses. He critiqued the previous "solid" approach as being a simplistic review of "what research participants say" during interviews, where the analysis of this data is often based on the identification of cultural facts, essentialized into themes that "give the impression of 'encounters of cultures' rather than individuals" (p. 38-9). Dervin claimed that we need to see the multidimensionality of individuals' acculturation and identity as people interact and move across cultural spaces. Part of this involves searching for "hidden discourses," not just relying on what the research participant says but also listening for the "other" voices that are involved in participants' construction of the experience. Complex sociocultural experiences should not be oversimplified or subject to cultural or linguistic essentialization if we are indeed aspiring to orient ourselves to the experiences of diverse groups within our educational communities.

Entering Curricular Contexts

As noted previously, while the enrollment of international students is often highlighted as a core component of internationalization and is thought to enhance the diversity profile of the campus, this loose perception of benefit is often combined with an attitude of assimilation when we look at L2 students' experiences within curricular settings. In fact, despite this diverse new reality on our campuses, multilingualism in our classrooms is often treated as "a problem to be solved, a disease to be cured" (Hall, 2009, p. 37). It is a challenge to cultivate global-mindedness in U.S. classrooms if they remain monocultural and operate "in isolation of the wider world and where the student body, staff, curriculum context and supporting materials all reflect a single dominant culture" (Caruana, 2010, p. 34). A good deal of the relevant literature notes the superficial ways in which many institutions regard international students, from culturally essentializing perceptions (Benesch, 1993; Hinkel, 1999; Kubota, 2001; McKay, 1993; Morita, 2004; Pennycook, 1994; Raimes, 1991; Singh & Doherty, 2004; Spack, 1997b; Zamel, 1995, 1997; Zamel & Spack, 2004) to the labels that derive from institutional placement policies (Chiang & Schmida, 2006; Costino & Hyon, 2007; Harklau, 2000; Ortmeier-Hooper, 2008; Spack, 1997b; Zamel, 1997).

Research on faculty views of L2 students has also highlighted a deficit perception, as well as a tendency to judge L2 students' "cognitive and intellectual development from the stance of the monolingual culture" (Spack, 2004, p. 37). Such assumptions not only devalue the rich and unique backgrounds of international students but also disregard the fact that these students come from diverse and equally strong epistemological traditions and have been influenced by their own sociocultural histories. Even if members of the mainstream institutional community respect and are inclusive of L2 students, an overall perception of difference often remains (Kubota, 2001) and faculty may feel ill-equipped to respond to the needs of L2 students in their classes (Ferris, Brown, Liu, & Stine, 2011; Matsuda, Saenkhum, & Accardi, 2013).

Regardless of the existing infrastructure or institutional attitudes toward diversity, international students who enroll in U.S. colleges and universities are expected to meet the same degree requirements as mainstream American students. According to the Conference on College Composition and Communication (CCCC) "Statement on Second Language Writing and Writers," the presence of second language students in our composition classrooms is the new reality, and institutions need to acknowledge this fact and work "to understand their characteristics, and to develop instructional and institutional practices that are sensitive to their linguistic and cultural needs" (Matsuda et al., 2006, p. 11). Part of this ethical responsibility involves stepping back to consider the confluence of factors that influence a student's experience in U.S. classrooms and acknowledging the fact that the U.S. college curriculum is not ideologically neutral (Berlin, 1988; Canagarajah, 2002; Dean, 1989; Horner, 2006; Horner & Trimbur, 2002; Martin-Jones & Heller, 1996; Matsuda, 2006, 2012; Ramanathan & Atkinson, 1999; Santos, 1992, 2001; Silva, Leki, & Carson, 1997). Curricular practices, such as elite institutions' recent trend of offering rigorous, thematically oriented first-year writing courses to undergraduate students, have the potential to be inclusive and promote global and cross-cultural engagement. However, if the content assumes practical and cultural knowledge that is inherently "American" or "Western," L2 writers from other traditions may feel silenced or isolated from the material and their peers.

There is a fairly well-developed research base on the experiences of L2 students as writers across the U.S. college curriculum, with much of it focused on literacy demands, language acquisition/use, and composing processes (Carson, 2001; Carson, Chase, Gibson, & Hargrove, 1992; Cumming, 2001; Ferris, 1998; Ferris & Tagg, 1996; Ginther & Grant, 1996; Hinkel, 2002, 2005; Huang, 2010; Leki & Carson, 1994, 1997; Leki, Cumming, & Silva, 2008; Raimes, 1987; Silva, 1993). Indeed, much of the research that addresses the inclusion of L2 writers in mainstream settings focuses on how L2 students develop their English language proficiency or their capacity to write in an academic setting—in other words, the practical negotiation of the expectations of the new academic literacy community. Such research is incredibly valuable and has advanced both understandings and pedagogical practices but at the same time tends to focus on a particular aspect of students' experiences, rather than taking a holistic view that includes the totality of factors that shape their experience in the mainstream classroom. Longitudinal case studies of students' experiences as writers have had the benefit of providing deeper narrative insights (Angelova & Riazantseva, 1999; Carroll, 2002; Fu, 1995; Hsieh, 2007; Leki, 1995, 2007; Morita, 2004; Smoke, 1994, 2004; Spack, 1997a, 2004; Zhou, Knoke, & Sakamoto, 2005). Leki's study, in particular, made a strong case for expanding research agendas beyond the development of language skills by situating research in a perspective that better reflects L2 students' "lived academic experiences" (p. 282) and is inclusive of the role that linguistic, social, cultural, and ideological elements play. Many of the cited studies, including Leki's, illuminate the challenges and successes undergraduate students experience writing in the context of courses across the curriculum.

Making Sense of First-Year Writing

More narrowly, research is increasingly exploring how L2 undergraduate students in U.S. higher education make sense of being a part of the ubiquitous first-year writing requirement. Fleming (2011) called this particular course the "most required, most taught, and the most taken course in U.S. higher education" (p. 1), first offered at Harvard almost 150 years ago and becoming ubiquitous by 1900. Interesting to the study at hand, the initial impetus for this required writing course was linked to the need for students to have a communicative command of the U.S. "mother tongue" as the country rapidly industrialized. As time went on, despite changes in schooling practices, technological advances, and growing diversity, the first-year writing requirement has remained a staple of higher education curricula. Though arrangements across institutions may vary, Fleming described the core of the requirement as a "stand-alone course in expository writing at the college level" that assesses and promotes literacy skills near students' point of entry into the academic community (p. 3). Despite its ubiquity and purpose, however, this course has tended to emphasize a set of generalizable *skills*, initially motivated by a public perception of a literacy crisis caused by higher education's failure to teach students to write properly. In addition, according to Crowley (1998), the "composition classroom" is often represented as a generic entity, a similarly constructed space regardless of setting, "as if the politics of class, status, and location were not operative in our classrooms" (p. 222). This notion of the generic classroom is one that I wanted to interrogate in my study.

Much of this history of the composition course was echoed in Beaufort's (2007) book *College Writing and Beyond: A New Framework for University Writing Instruction*. While she asserted that writing is a complex social and intellectual activity that has a great potential for motivating learning, in many ways this requirement remains an "isolated course, an end in itself" (p. 9). Such writing courses are seen as important enough to be compulsory, but instructors are often seen as generalists who lack disciplinary grounding and are often low-status contingent faculty (Beaufort, 2007; Crowley, 1998; Fleming, 2011). In addition, the skills taught may have the appearance of being transferable but are often so generic that they have little applicability in the various discourse communities students will enter in their later years of study. In terms of content, the typical first-year writing course emphasizes skills over content, often drawing on a "smorgasbord of readings . . . which keeps the level of engagement with ideas and information more superficial" (Beaufort, 2007, p. 12). With literacy as the core goal, many writing programs in U.S. colleges and universities operate outside of disciplinary knowledge domains and institutional structures; in other words, they tend not to be affiliated with traditional disciplines in academia, and instruction is often focused on "form," rather than content or meaning (Beaufort, 2007; Crowley, 1998; Matsuda, 2012). This institutional assumption often relegates writing courses to the academic margins, despite the compulsory nature of the curricular requirement.

In recent decades, the traditional paradigm of first-year writing, including its treatment of L2 students, has been challenged by the work of a growing cadre of composition-rhetoric and L2 writing scholars, as well as by innovations in institutional arrangements, such as the creation of writing departments that may combine FYW with writing across the curriculum (WAC) or writing in the disciplines (WID) programs. Not only is writing more embedded across undergraduate curricula but FYW is increasingly characterized by sustained interaction with interdisciplinary content. Thus in many ways, one of the core limitations of the field of writing instruction—its disconnect from the core disciplinary domains of the academy—has been converted into an opportunity. This aligns with Fleming's (2011) point that because writing courses are not "tethered to a traditional academic discipline," they do not have to instruct students through a "particular body of knowledge" (p. 14) and can therefore take on activity-based formats that can help students learn to write along the conventions of the academy while drawing on their own backgrounds and aspirations and linking these to their understanding of the wider world.

It should be noted here, however, that first-year writing—as a required curricular element—is inexorably tied to American ideological notions of politics, culture, and society (Berlin, 1988), which is a significant factor when considering the experiences of L2 international students in our classrooms. At the same time, there is a notably postmodern emphasis within writing programs in the United States, in which writing is considered the "product of social and material conditions" (Berlin, 1992, p. 18) and where "students must come to see that the languages they are expected to speak, write, and embrace as ways of thinking and acting are never disinterested" (p. 24). Hence, it can be said that the FYW requirement is in many ways an American phenomenon that has been institutionalized through the higher education system.

Though some FYW courses continue to operate on a relatively generic model—for example, using a textbook reader and asking students to write a series of short topical essays, or offering parallel, and likely more remedial, FYW sections for L2 students—the literature has outlined several options that innovate curricular arrangements to include L2 writers, including cross-cultural sections of writing courses (Ibrahim & Penfield, 2005; Matsuda & Silva, 1999) and the newer trend of writing-about-writing (Downs & Wardle, 2007). A number of institutions have also transitioned their generic first-year composition sequences into more rigorous literacy sequences that combine theme-based FYW classes with WID or WAC courses (Matsuda, 2012). Despite this emphasis on writing's relationship to content, it should be noted that Matsuda and Silva (1999) warned that content should not be prioritized over writing instruction in such classes, despite any instructor's vested interest in a particular topic or content area. The history of first-year writing is significant because the requirement to complete this course is one of the few academic experiences that nearly every student enrolled in any program of study—L1 or L2—goes through. Although it is technically a course that is focused on skill and form, it still has powerful potential for content and meaning-based interactions and is a worthy site of research into diverse students' lived experience in U.S. higher education.

New Ways to Conceptualize the Experience: This Study

The myriad and complex factors that influence L2 students' experiences in U.S. higher education demand new conceptualizations that are grounded in research. Hence, a significant purpose of this study is to shed light on the internationalization of higher education by developing a deeper understanding of L2 students' "lived experience" within a particular socio-academic setting: a required mainstream first-year writing class in a U.S. university. For the purposes of this research, *socio-academic space* represents a shared environment where course content and formal academic tasks are combined with mediated social interactions among members of the classroom community, all of whom carry with them their unique sociocultural histories and perspectives. This investigation was motivated by my desire to develop a "complex, detailed understanding" of this phenomenon (Creswell, 2007, p. 43) as it is experienced and made sense of by my participants. The research was ethically situated on several levels. First, if U.S. institutions are to continue to recruit and enroll international students, they have a responsibility to develop a deeper awareness of the students' experiences within the institutional and curricular frameworks. Further, to truly link internationalization policy to the practice of global engagement, schools need to be reflective of the experiences of culturally and linguistically diverse students in their classrooms and of how they can create more purposeful and sustained opportunities for cross-cultural learning. This understanding comes not from making assumptions about who we think these students are but from orienting ourselves to their experiences as related in their own voices.

I selected a classroom setting that was both ubiquitous and unique as the site of this research because it is an early and formative experience in students' academic careers. In addition, first-year writing classes that take a thematic approach are often grounded in rich and culturally complex content, yet the conventions that govern academic writing align with Western conventions of argumentation, rhetorical awareness, and epistemology.

Further, there is a general expectation that entering this academic literacy community requires active engagement on the part of students; in other words, the writing classroom is not a space where students can sit passively and absorb knowledge. As the number of students who come from different educational and writing traditions continues to grow in U.S. mainstream classrooms, developing new ways of understanding their experiences is imperative.

Part of this understanding depends on taking a more robust view of L2 students' experiences, including how course materials, instructional approaches and tasks, participant backgrounds and beliefs, and classroom interactions combine to inform the classroom experience. As Zamel (2000) emphasized, we need to "view each classroom as a culture in its own right—a culture with its own norms, conventions, expectations—and to understand that it is the process of working within this classroom that makes it possible for participants to acquire its discourse" (p. 9). Leki's (2006) consideration of socio-academic relations between faculty and students, as well as the work of Villamil and Guerrero (2006) and Nelson and Carson (2006) on peer interactions, further sheds light on the extent to which classroom-based relationships shape students' experiences. Paltridge, Starfield, and Tardy's (2016) recent advocacy for research that applies an ethnographic lens to academic writing further supports a broadening of how we study culturally and linguistically diverse students in U.S. higher education. Taking into account the totality of L2 students' experience in mainstream classrooms also resonates with the work of Shapiro, Cox, Shuck, and Simnitt (2016), who argue that we need to go beyond "appreciation" and "inclusion" of diverse students and begin to recognize and promote their agency in U.S. college classrooms.

Beyond the classroom, the research elucidated in this book has potential significance in several key areas. First, the findings add dimension to overall understandings of internationalization trends and institutional agendas. Much of the present research in this area emphasizes trends in international student flows, institutional policies toward internationalization, or acculturation

studies that measure the extent to which L2 students adapt to
the existing socio-academic environment. Yet if the internationalization of higher education and the development of global
competencies is a goal institutions want to realize, they must
think about the "spaces" in which these transformations actually occur.

This study bridges big-picture policy notions about internationalization with the on-the-ground reality for L2 students
who are being recruited and enrolled in order to advance internationalization agendas. Mainstream classrooms, where L2 students interact with L1 students, are sites of global engagement
and can help to assess what internationalization initiatives
mean in practice. Part of this will necessarily require a questioning of assumptions, both those that underlie the literature
of internationalization and those that shape attitudes and practices at an institutional level. U.S. colleges and universities cannot assume that they know who their L2 students are, not only
because their "profile" has changed compared to previous generations of international students (Choudaha, Orosz, & Chang,
2012; Fischer, 2011), but also because these students themselves
are products of a globally interconnected—and transnationally
mobile—society. As Rizvi (2005) noted, this mobility does not
render these students culture-less but adds a new "cosmopolitan" dimension to our understanding of them, "underpinned by
a more dynamic view of cultural identity that emerges out of the
conditions of global interculturality; and of critical engagement
with ideas and images that circulate around the world" (p. 334).
This is an exciting new space from which to consider both the
global and the local.

This point ties neatly to colleges' and universities' penchant
for actively pursuing internationalization, as well as the institutional rhetoric frequently deployed about the importance of
deep and transformative global and cross-cultural student learning. Even if our ambitions are not so lofty, this study is a step
toward helping us acknowledge the diverse values and perspectives within our own institutions by taking into account those
who might be excluded or marginalized by existing institutional

practices. Developing cross-cultural understanding and effective practices in regard to international students will also go far in enhancing the long-term reputation of U.S. institutions and even maintaining positive diplomatic relations among nations. As political climates and global mobility patterns shift, maintaining a positive reputation will become even more important.

The findings of this study also have implications on a curricular and pedagogical level. Exploring the lived experiences of L2 students in U.S. classrooms shines a light on teaching and learning practices. On many levels, the existing literature highlights the fact that L2 students tend to be viewed through a deficit lens by administrators, faculty, and even fellow students. In addition, in light of the growing emphasis on global engagement and global competency, schools need to reexamine status quo curricular and pedagogical approaches. The findings of this study motivate administrators and faculty to think in new ways about how student diversity can be tapped as a resource for cultivating global competency (Siczek, 2015; Straker, 2016; Urban & Palmer, 2014); as Jones and Killick (2007) have emphasized, diversity among students is "the most obvious, and perhaps least utilized" mechanism for improving teaching and learning for global purposes (p. 113). In fact, international students and students from diverse backgrounds are particularly equipped to develop global competencies and global mindedness by the very experience of their transnational migration: They themselves have crossed cultural, linguistic, and epistemological boundaries to be members of U.S. college communities.

Because diverse students are members of mainstream classrooms across American campuses, the findings of the study that this book is based on translate to educators across disciplines; however, as noted in the Introduction, the findings presented here are notably significant for writing programs and writing-intensive courses. Academic writing is a field that is governed by strict conventions in many aspects, but the potential for content engagement and critical thinking is high, particularly considering some of the recent curricular and instructional innovations and the increasing acknowledgment that multilingual and multicultural classrooms have become the norm in U.S. higher education (Hall, 2014). Understanding the experience of culturally and linguistically diverse students, including how they interpret content and interactions in this academic literacy community, allows educators to think in new ways about U.S. or Western approaches to knowledge, communication, and pedagogy—and perhaps to think in new ways about engaging both L2 and L1 students in U.S. classrooms.

Value of Sociocultural Perspectives and Hermeneutic Phenomenological Inquiry

The final section of this opening chapter articulates how and why this study was grounded in a particular set of research traditions. The basis of this inquiry was qualitative, in line with my desire as a situated researcher to understand how these ten participants, as L2 students, constructed and revealed their experiences in a mainstream academic writing class. Qualitative research was the most powerful vehicle for this study because its primary concern is "the world of lived experience . . . where individual belief and action intersect with culture" (Denzin & Lincoln, 2000, p. 8). Perhaps more deeply, this approach illuminated the deep relationship between me as a researcher and what I was studying. Van Manen (1990) emphasized that a "certain dialectic" should exist between a research question and a methodological approach, and I was powerfully moved by his point that the method chosen should be in "harmony with the deep interest that makes one an educator in the first place" (p. 2).

The hermeneutic phenomenological approach originated from a particular epistemological root, which emphasizes my general orientation toward life and how I believe knowledge is derived: We shape our lifeworld and our world simultaneously shapes us, and through *intentional* interpretation we can reach new understandings of particular social realities, capturing "how social experience is created and given meaning" (Denzin & Lincoln, 2000, p. 10). We must acknowledge that social phenomena are complex and that our understanding of these issues is often socially constructed and interpretive, which further motivated my decision to use a hermeneutic phenomenological approach for this study: I sought to understand the nature of this lived experience because, as van Manen (1990) argued, we cannot take the pedagogies that we engage with as educators for granted; instead we must open ourselves up to understanding the phenomenon in question as it is revealed by those who experience it directly.

In line with a phenomenological approach, the epistemological tradition that informed this project was constructivism, which involves the belief that knowledge is generated and shared in a social context. This framework thus centers on meaning making, and the researcher is called upon to listen to the participants to get a full sense of the often complex and subjective meanings that are derived from their social and cultural histories as well as their interactions with others. This research was more narrowly situated within the paradigm of social constructionism, which emphasizes the role of language and power in this negotiated terrain. Other theoretical influences conceptually embedded in this research were Vygotskyian sociocultural theory and activity theory, both of which have been linked to research across educational settings, particularly in the field of composition studies. Language learning, in this case L2 writing, is situated in a particular context and mediated through classroom interactions surrounding the course content.

While quantitative research in education may have the benefit of being hypothesized, experimentally controlled, and generalizable in its attempt to identify "what is true for one and all" (van Manen, 1990, p. 6), phenomenological approaches are grounded in the lifeworld of lived experiences. In fact, hermeneutic phenomenology, in van Manen's words, can be seen as a "philosophy of the personal, the individual, which we pursue against the backdrop of an understanding of the evasive character of the logos of other, the whole, the communal, or the social" (p. 7). This is a rich vantage point from which to develop an understanding of one's experiences in educational settings, particularly when participants may be on the linguistic and cultural margins of the dominant community. For the purposes of this book, I'd like to emphasize that though certain epistemological concerns guide such research, we must not remain only in this rarified territory; van Manen (1990) called for us to remember that we are "interested in the pedagogic praxis" (p. 8) of our educational research, and that, as such, we aim to increase the thoughtfulness and purposefulness in our pedagogic activities.

2

Meet the Participants

In many important ways, this project is premised on the situated nature of humans' response to new experiences. This situatedness is in part historical, shaped by what has been called our *forestructure*: We enter new contexts carrying our sociocultural history and make sense of new experiences through a process of negotiating where we come from, who we are, and what we know and understand within a new set of experiences and interactions.

This chapter focuses on participants' lives prior to entering the mainstream U.S. classroom setting and reminds us that the participants are individuals and sentient beings, not statistical evidence of diversity or internationalization or representatives of some monolithic cultural or linguistic background. The chapter includes a series of descriptive vignettes based on participant self-description and researcher-written memos immediately following the first set of interviews for the study. At the time the data were collected, all participants were in their first year of study at the U.S. university, and they selected their own pseudonyms for the purposes of the research.

Participant Vignettes

Han Gil

Han Gil, an 18-year-old Korean from the business school, had a high level of conversational fluency, largely as a result of the seven years he spent at a boarding school in India. When asked about his interests or hobbies, the only personal detail he shared was playing musical instruments, including the piano and a "Japanese xylophone," which he did not bring with him to the U.S. because it was "the size of a truck." I would describe Han Gil as having a strong sense of self; he appeared focused on what he needed to get done and came across as independently minded. At the same time, he used powerful and strong language to describe the ways he saw some negative aspects of Korean culture reproduced in his peer relationships abroad. Each time I spoke with Han Gil, I was struck by how clearly he expressed the future he wanted for himself and his perceived sense of agency in the choices he was making.

Han Gil grew up in a town near the center of South Korea, and his "entire family" worked in the field of social work. His father earned a PhD from a U.S. university and his mother was a university professor; he had two younger brothers—one just a year younger and the other eleven years younger. When describing the role of his family in his life, he expressed particular respect for his grandfather, who came from an extremely poor family with seven children: "He was the second one and the family was only able to offer the first one to study." Despite these challenges, his grandfather saved money, bought land, and "created a village" to support those poorer than himself. Han Gil described this village as a "comfortable city" with "no beggars" and "no strangers." Today, more than one thousand people—including "orphans, old people, and mentally ill people"—are living there. Han Gil spent a lot of time in this community and demonstrated entrepreneurial tendencies by opening his own small business in Korea, a dog "hair salon" and hotel.

Because education was considered so important to his family, Han Gil was sent to the city to attend a high-quality elementary school. Perhaps the most visible representation of his family's commitment to education was the decision to send Han Gil to India for boarding school starting in the fifth grade. Initially he did not want to go, and he admittedly struggled in his early years there; in fact, upon his arrival he said he could not even write his name in English and that he was miserable, homesick, and bullied by his peers. In the end, however, he said that his experience in India broadened his horizons and prepared him for his study in the U.S. Han Gil was not particularly excited about attending college in the U.S. ("I just felt like I am going into same cycle again") and said his "only concern [was] about academics." There was something highly pragmatic in Han Gil's view of studying abroad; he saw a U.S. education as an investment in his future.

Crystal

Crystal was a Chinese woman, who at the age of 21 was one of the older participants, having transferred from what she called a "famous" Chinese university. She entered the U.S. university as a junior, studying event management in the business school. She was extremely open to sharing her experiences and opinions; in fact, she provided answers to a number of my listed questions before the first interview had even officially begun—her experiences and feelings simply tumbling out of her mouth. Though her father, who worked in government industry, was less involved in her life, she described her mother, a sixth grade teacher, as having a loving and powerful influence on her life: "My mother obviously did a lot for me . . . my mom just wanted me to see more."

Crystal grew up speaking Chinese at home and completed all of her schooling in her hometown. Initially, she had not wanted to attend the university in her hometown because she "grew up there" and found it "too familiar," and noted that she did not like the school's appearance ("I think the school's gate was so ugly!"), but because her exam score was high enough to matriculate in one of the top programs, she decided to attend the university in her hometown. Though Crystal did not originally intend to study in the U.S. or transfer, she was told that her father's colleague's daughter was transferring to a U.S. university, which inspired the decision for Crystal to eventually matriculate there. Despite the fact that this had not been part of her plan, she said she was happy to get away from her hometown university, emphasizing that she wanted to "see more" and "to live by myself." She also had a strong critique of the event management program at her former university and knew that if she wanted to go to graduate school in the U.S., she would need a better education, including a stronger command of English. According to Crystal, the U.S. had better undergraduate programs and attending one would improve her chances of getting admitted to a graduate program in her desired field of study. Before moving to the U.S., she perceived the U.S. classroom environment to be full of discussion and group work, with a free and relaxed atmosphere. Interestingly, however, once she matriculated, she said she had actually felt more free in a Chinese university because there it was the "same students, same classes, same program."

Once the decision was made for her to study abroad, she said that she felt "so relaxed" and, upon arrival in the U.S., when she was met at the airport by some members of a local Christian church, that she felt happy and free. The transition, however, was harder than she expected: "I thought it shouldn't be that hard." She got sick as soon as she arrived and went through early struggles, describing herself as homesick, lonely, and having a hard time making friends ("I just don't like partying."). After one semester, Crystal found her place in the university community, but the rawness of her emotion when talking about her initial transition—as well as the honesty with which she shared her story throughout all of the interviews—made her a compelling participant.

Ai

Ai was a 19-year-old business school student who had attended a public middle and high school in his hometown of Guangzhou, China, and grew up speaking Cantonese at home and Mandarin as the "official" second language everyone learned. My first impression of Ai was that he was cheerful and optimistic, a young man with a positive outlook on life and a determination to persevere. In fact, he said he chose the pseudonym "Ai" because it means "love." He described himself as having lots of friends and being active in China but thought that China—and his high school classes there—were too "huge" and that he was "missing something." Though he was an only child, he initiated the family conversation about doing an exchange program in Minnesota, and his parents supported this decision.

Ai's father owned a business that imported and exported alcohol, and his mother was a former cosmetologist; according to Ai, they had not had opportunities like this (to study abroad), but cousins and family friends had, so it was not beyond the family's scope of understanding. Ai's family had also traveled abroad quite a bit, even visiting the U.S. before he joined his exchange program. Though he had only intended to spend his junior year of high school as an exchange student, Ai decided to remain in Minnesota for his senior year. He described his transition to a U.S. Catholic high school as hard at first. He felt "saddened" and "really nervous" at the beginning because, as he said, "I'm not sure what the outside world looked like and I didn't know if I have good English skills to communicate with others." Ai was the only Chinese student in his school, but he made good friends and liked his teachers and host family. Though he said "I don't have religion in China," he said he found Catholicism "really interesting to study." Such statements convey what I would call Ai's overriding characteristics: openness, determination, and generosity.

Because his parents did not speak English well, Ai researched U.S. schooling options independently and strategically, and rankings and prestige factored into his decision about which universities to apply to and what he wanted to study. He said that his parents financially supported him but emphasized that he was "a big boy already," having left home alone at 17. Ai had a clear memory of saying goodbye at the airport when he was leaving for college; he had to "turn [his] face away" so as not to see his parents cry, but as he moved to the security check he said, "OK . . . my journey begins."

John

John, age 19, was also a business school student, born and raised in Ecuador. He grew up speaking Spanish at home and attended all grades at the same school, graduating from an

English-medium International Baccalaureate (IB) program at
the local high school. In interviews, he came across as mature
and self-possessed, and he had a high level of oral fluency in
English. His responses to interview questions tended to be well
developed and thoughtful, and he projected a reflective open-
mindedness. Though he described himself as "shy," he also said,
"When I am in confidence, I start talking." John also described
himself as a "planner" who liked structure and tried to "minimize struggles." It was clear in each interview that friends and
family were extremely important to him, both in his life in Ecuador and in his life at the U.S. university.

John described his family as being from the "upper class"
and running a successful family business in the shrimp industry. He said that his mother used to have a career but became a
stay-at-home mom to take care of him and his younger brothers.
After graduating high school, John spent eight months working
in the family business, where he said he was treated more like
an employee than a relative, except when it came to meals; his
only "privilege," he said, was lunch because his family knew
what a picky eater he was. His home space was shared with
extended family. John's closeness to his family was emphasized
at multiple points during the interviews: "We're really spoiled.
We're really together, and it's hard to go apart." John was also
well traveled internationally, but did not take these opportunities for granted ("I had that blessing that I have been around
the world a lot."). Like Han Gil, he idolized his grandfather who
only had a third grade education and started his own business
from nothing: "That's why I want to start my own company. . . .
to have my own legacy." John also expressed admiration for his
father, who spoke five languages and had lived all over Europe.

John noted that it had been his own idea to come to the
States; he knew it would be hard but that he "had this idea"
from a young age that he wanted to go abroad, and his parents
supported him and helped move the process forward. When
it came time for him to depart for university, his mother and
godmother accompanied him. His commitment to his family
was further displayed when, just a couple of months into the

semester, he flew back to Ecuador for the first communion of his youngest brother, whom he called "the jewel in the crown" of his family and "the most spoiled kid you're ever going to meet. Everybody loves him."

Amy

Amy, 18, was a woman from Beijing who had attended what she called a "typical Chinese school" with a competitive focus on academics. She matriculated into the international affairs school at the U.S. university. She came across as very open to the research, as well as poised, thoughtful, and well spoken. She was receptive and genuine in speaking about her experiences and was a star participant insofar as she tied her description to particular instances and anecdotes. Amy described both of her parents as professional, with her mother holding a position in pharmaceutical sales and her father the "boss of a news agency" in the field of aeronautics. She was notably inspired by her father and his work, harboring an early dream for a career in aeronautics that led her to travel to Florida at the age of 13 to learn how to fly an airplane. Her father spoke English well because of his many international contacts, and the family was quite well traveled and hosted international visitors frequently.

A formative experience Amy described was when her father asked her to be a "tour guide" for a family friend, a college student visiting from Boston, when she was 15. She took all initiative for showing him around and taking him to Shanghai. Though she had spent "most of her life in China" and assumed she would go to college there, this experience opened her eyes to global options. Amy said it was her own idea to come to the States to study. She wanted to be independent and "to go to another place on my own," and she did not want to be "trapped in China." Though her mother was a bit more protective, her parents agreed they could afford to send her to university in the United States and were supportive of her decision. Her first real experience abroad, however, was a bit more stressful. She entered a pre-college summer program at an Ivy League university, which she described as overwhelming both academically and socially: "I was living in a suite with 15 native speakers . . . girls like talk really fast and then they talk together . . . they're really accepting and they really like me, but most times I cannot like understand all what they're saying so I just sit there." She said her experience in the summer pre-college program cast a "shadow" that made her worry if she could manage university study in the United States, but at the same time she was proud of herself and ready to take on the opportunity.

Lora

Lora was a 19-year-old Chinese woman who had attended a traditional high school of 4,000 students in the capital of inner Mongolia. She matriculated in the college of arts and sciences with an interest in studying interior design. She spoke Mandarin both at home and in school. Initially, Lora displayed a little reticence about being involved in the study, even emailing before the first interview to ask how to prepare and what gestures to use. At the end of the first interview, she seemed very pleased when I told her how well she had done and how helpful her responses were. In general, Lora was a little less chatty than the others—I would describe her as introverted and somewhat earnest—which meant I had to ask her more follow-up questions, but the responses she gave always came across as thoughtful and honest.

When asked about her family background, Lora said: "I'm an only child—that's common in China" and described her family as "normal." Her mother was a medical doctor, and her father managed a steel company. She did not share a lot of information about her interests and experiences prior to coming to the U.S. but did share a memory of a high school English speaking competition: "I was representing my class so it was kind of a big deal." Though she could not remember the topic about which she spoke, she remembered feeling excited because it was her "first time on the stage."

Before going abroad for university, Lora spent her whole life in her hometown, noting, "In my hometown, not many people go abroad to study." Her decision to study abroad was in part inspired by a visit from a family friend who lived in the U.S.—it made her feel the possibility of going there to study. Lora also knew teachers and classmates who had "traveled around" and she said, "I think that's amazing." She also felt that because schooling in China was singularly focused on university entrance, once students got to college, it was "useless"; in fact, she said "Chinese college is like kindergarten." Lora also wanted to "see the world," and her father strongly agreed that she should take the opportunity. Her mother was resistant but eventually agreed, a fact to which Lora was quite sensitive. She said: "I don't want to hurt her, so, but my father talked to her, so like finally he convinced her; so he supported me and I appreciate that." After that, Lora spent a year in Beijing and Shanghai preparing for the SAT® and TOEFL® and studying English. There she interacted with others who had been abroad and had seen the world. Her parents flew with her to school and when they said goodbye she felt "a little excited and a little sad." She was curious about what America was really like, but a bit worried about her safety.

Michelle

Michelle was a Mongolian woman, age 22, who had transferred from a Mongolian university to matriculate in the international affairs school. She was very soft-spoken but in a way revealed the most about her experience. For example, I asked follow-up questions here and there, but she volunteered details in a helpful way. Michelle seemed very sensitive and family oriented. She had attended a private school in Mongolia from kindergarten through high school and had started a humanities degree at a university in Mongolia. Michelle grew up speaking Mongolian at home and had studied Japanese and English as foreign languages in school. She spent five months studying abroad in Japan and living with a friend from home and "enjoy[ing] her life in Japan" greatly. In terms of hobbies, Michelle said she had played the piano for five years. When asked if she still played, she said: "Yeah, just sometimes when I get angry or something depressed, I just play like some melody that I know, but I am not professional."

Michelle said her father owned a "little frame company" and collected fine art as a hobby while her mother worked as an accountant at a private mining company. The family had experience traveling to China and Russia, as was common for Mongolians of her parents' generation, and Michelle had vivid memories of a trip to Russia when she was only three; "I remember my childhood very well," she said. She had one brother who had lived in the United States for five years and was married with two children. His experience helped motivate the family decision to send Michelle abroad for school. Like other participants, Michelle was extremely close to her family; in fact, her mother and brother and his family ended up moving to the U.S. to live with her after she spent a brief unhappy time living in the university dorm.

Kristen

Kristen was an 18-year-old Chinese student who had matriculated in the arts and sciences college but had not decided her major yet. Kristen presented an interesting narrative; she was a comfortable English speaker, and her wisdom and sense of humor came out in unexpected ways during the interviews. When Kristen was a child, her parents had spent two years living in the United States and working for a computer manufacturer while she lived with her grandparents. When they returned to China, her father started his own investment business and her mother went to work in a related field.

Kristen originally came to the United States as a high school exchange student in rural Iowa during her sophomore year. The decision to study abroad for high school was in part prompted by something her mother's friend had said and in part motivated by Kristen's own understanding that Chinese high schools were overwhelmingly oriented toward the university entrance exam. In China, she said, there are many exams and students only have to "memorize stuff." In Iowa, she stayed with a Christian family and attended Christian school, describing the first year as hard: "When I arrived had no idea . . . my English is not that good and I can't really understand what's in the class." There were only two

Koreans and one Chinese student in her school, which promoted easier access to the local community. As Kristen said, "When there's less Chinese people, it's more easy to get into the circle of American students," and she described the people in her community as friendly and helpful. She continued as an exchange student for her senior year of high school, but decided to move to New Jersey, where she had a homestay with a Jewish family—encountering cultural differences that she found quite illuminating. After completing her high school in the United States, Kristen had no desire to attend university in China and systematically evaluated a number of U.S. universities before settling on the school she chose. Her initial arrival was not particularly stressful because she has already traveled alone to Iowa at the age of 15, though she characterized university life as different from her high school homestay because she had to do everything "by herself."

Yoono

Yoono was an 18-year-old Lebanese man who came to a U.S. university from Beirut to study civil engineering. I would say that Yoono had a very Westernized demeanor—he spoke English naturally and with a high level of fluency in English, immediately noting that he had gone to an international school. In terms of his linguistic background, Yoono said that at home and in society, he spoke a mixture of Arabic and English, though he was also proficient in French. In Lebanon, he noted, it is not uncommon for middle- to upper-class citizens to speak English fairly fluently and have a great deal of access to English language media and entertainment. In addition, his parents had studied and worked in the U.S. and he—both with his family and on his own—had traveled abroad extensively. In fact, he said he spent considerable time in Los Angeles when he was growing up because his grandparents had moved there 30 years earlier at the time of the Lebanese Civil War. He said he had two younger brothers, one of whom was autistic, and both of his parents were engineers. As far as hobbies, Yoono described himself as an athlete, regularly skiing, playing soccer, and participating in water sports: "I do a lot of stuff to keep in shape."

When he talked about his high school experience, he explained his motivation to apply for a rigorous International Baccalaureate (IB) program, rather than other available tracks, in this way: "I chose IB because I knew I wanted to study in the States." He thought it demonstrated to universities that he was willing to challenge himself. This strong sense of direction characterized Yoono's responses to questions throughout the interviews: He knew he wanted to study engineering and put plans in motion early to achieve this goal. His overall approach is perhaps best encapsulated in this quote: "I just wanted to make sure I can set myself up in the best way to do well."

When he learned he had been accepted at one of his top-choice universities in the U.S., he "felt really happy" and said, "I opened [the letter] and I read it and then I saw that I got in, and I rushed in to my mom's room and it was like 1:00 AM and she was sleeping 'cause there is a time difference; so yeah, I just rushed in to her room and I told her and she was really happy." Yoono described his initial transition to U.S. higher education as smooth; a couple of months later, however, he admitted becoming homesick, describing his feelings in this way: "When I would be alone or like before I would be going to bed, I would just think of times in Lebanon or just trying to imagine what the place looks like." Having said that, overall Yoono seemed confident, cosmopolitan, and adaptable—as evidenced by the fact that he seemed to gravitate toward a peer group of similarly global and cosmopolitan students.

Luca

Luca was a Colombian student who was 19 years old. Though Luca and her family spoke Spanish at home, she had been in a French school system all her life. She was studying international affairs at the U.S. university. I would describe Luca as chatty and personable, open and enthusiastic. Luca was originally from Bogota, but family circumstances prevented them from remaining there, and she, her parents, and her two sisters moved to the Dominican Republic when she was 13. Her father had started a business in the security industry, and her mother ran a baking company and later became a stay-at-home mom. When Luca was in high school, her father decided to expand his company into the United States, in part for the business opportunity but in large part for his daughters' future education. They moved to Bethesda, Maryland, where Luca and her sisters enrolled in a local French school, which she found to be more challenging than the French school she had attended in the Dominican Republic: "Even though we were in the same school, like the same system, it was harder; you needed more discipline, um, you were not in an island any more like this was in the U.S. so yeah. I kind of grow up here a little bit more." She describes herself as multilingual, with Spanish as her first language, French as her second language, and English as her third language—and she had even begun to study Portuguese.

Though she had traveled to the United States—including Disney World—a number of times, she said, "It's different to come to visit for the holidays than living in the place." She noted that upon moving to Maryland, she found herself taking on more adult responsibilities for the family. Luca seemed tightly connected to her family and had a particular admiration for her father and his work. Before even starting university, she had worked as an assistant in her father's company, and she had a desire to study conflict resolution so that she could follow her dad into the company. "I just am proud of it [her father's work] . . . and I would love to continue my work in his legacy." Though the university she selected was not far from her family's home, she opted to live on campus, which she described as a "tough step for my parents because in Latin America, we don't have that culture"; even if you went two hours away for college, she said, "You didn't, like, sleep in there." But she convinced her parents to let her live in the dorm and come home on weekends. I would describe Luca as naturally sociable and, though she took her responsibilities seriously, she had a candid and open and somewhat lighthearted manner of interacting at times.

This chapter is a brief introduction to each of the ten L2 students who were willing to share their experiences and insights with me. In many ways, their words and voices create this story, and it is through their contributions that we can enter into their worlds and deepen our understanding of their experiences as international students.

Global Mobility and Higher Education

This chapter contextualizes the phenomenon of transnational migration for higher education and explores the sociocultural space out of which these ten participants were "projected." I consider this part of the forestructure that influenced their socio-academic experience in the FYW classroom. It involves developing an understanding of L2 students' sociocultural and family backgrounds and their individual experiences as they relate to pursuing higher education abroad.

The Phenomenon of Transnational Mobility for Higher Education

As previously mentioned, the *Open Doors* report on global study mobility is a frequently cited reference for statistics on international student enrollments in the United States, which estimated that more than a million international students studied at U.S. higher educational institutions in 2015–2016 (Institute of International Education, 2016). Similarly, according to a report on attitudes and perceptions about global higher education, the United States has overwhelmingly been the destination of choice for international students; the majority of respondents perceived the United States as having the highest quality education, the widest range of schools and programs, and the most welcoming environment for international students (Chow, 2011). It is projected that the United States will continue to be a top destination

Figure 3.1: Sociocultural History and Transnational Mobility

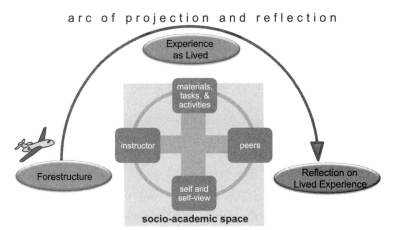

for international students in the decades to come, with China, India, and Saudi Arabia expected to fuel a large part of this growth (Fischer, 2013). It should be noted, however, that as political and immigration contexts shift, these enrollment patterns may no longer hold true.

The literature on international students' motivation to migrate often emphasizes that a combination of "push-pull" factors motivate the decision to study abroad (Altbach, 2004; Chirkov et al., 2007; Chow, 2011; Lee, 2008; Mazzarol & Soutar, 2002). *Push factors* are specific to conditions within the home country or family environment, such as economic or political conditions, or a family's commitment to a quality education. *Pull factors* are characterized by some perception of benefit from an education in the host country abroad, such as the perceived quality of its educational environment or the opportunities that would follow from earning a degree there. Mazzarol and Soutar (2002) identified six factors that influence an international student's decision to study abroad in a particular host country:

1. level of knowledge or awareness of host country
2. personal referrals and recommendations
3. cost issues

4. environment
5. geographic proximity
6. social links

Bodycott's (2009) research in a mainland Chinese context highlighted the fact that parents and students related different motivations for attending a university abroad. Parents seemed most concerned with the competitive university environment in China and the pragmatic opportunities created by an education abroad, such as better employment opportunities. Students, however, emphasized the desire for a "high-quality" education that included international and intercultural experiences and a more open educational system than the one available in China.

Chen (2008) analyzed data from two studies in a Canadian context to find that, in addition to the more traditional push-pull factors, undergraduates tended to be strongly influenced by family in the decision to study abroad, but that the decision of which institution to attend was informed on a more personal level, shaped by messaging about the school. Chen made note of the "blurred" distinction between internationalization agendas and marketing domains, claiming that though academics may eschew the "corporatization of higher education," strategic branding and marketing allows institutions to "survive in an increasingly competitive environment" (p. 6). Lee (2008) added further dimension to understandings of college access on a global scale by exploring the sources of information that influenced international students' choice of institution. Though information was gathered from a variety of sources, the most influential factor in school choice was considered the reputation of the institution, regardless of how much or how little was actually known about the setting of the school itself.

Recent research by Choudaha, Orosz, and Chang (2012) of World Education Services offered a new perspective on the profile of international students who study abroad; the report's key finding was that the international student population is extremely heterogeneous. The research team examined survey data on approximately 1,600 students from 115 countries and considered their academic aspirations, habits, and finances. They established four main categories of international students: *strivers*, who have high educational goals but may lack resources; *strugglers*, who tend to be poorly prepared both academically and financially; *explorers*, who are less prepared academically but well-financed; and *highfliers*, who are prepared both academically and financially. This research was tied to marketing and recruitment efforts and provided valuable information about the main countries that send students to the United States (China, South Korea, India), as well as the information channels these students used to make decisions about higher education abroad. Fischer (2011) also noted that old assumptions about "who" international students on U.S. campuses are no longer hold true: Incoming international students are likely to be younger, come from burgeoning middle-class backgrounds in countries like China and South Korea, and have less of a sense of direction when it comes to their academic aspirations. Research on shifts in mobility patterns and student profiles is a reminder of the danger of assuming a one-size-fits-all approach to developing institutional policies and practices and helps justify research that seeks to understand international students' lived experiences in U.S. institutional settings.

Participant Contexts for Transnational Mobility

A Diverse Participant Profile

Data from the first set of interviews for the study was used to characterize participants' context for transnational migration—in other words, the circumstances and decisions that motivated their decision to pursue an undergraduate degree at a U.S. university. The most notable early finding of this study was testament to the wide diversity among this international student population. All of the students who agreed to participate in the study met the criteria of being matriculated international undergraduates who spoke English as a second or additional language; however, their response to initial questions about

their backgrounds emphasizes the diverse sociocultural histories these students carry into our institutions. Though not sta-
tistically representative, the study sample reflected a balance
of participants in terms of gender, country of origin, language
background, and program of study. Although female participants outnumbered male participants in the study, this is in
line with the gender ratio of the research site, where approximately 55 percent of the undergraduate student population was
female. The balance of geographical and linguistic diversity
also aligns relatively well with the overall distribution of international undergraduates at the research site, as well as across
the United States (Institute of International Education, 2013).
Half of the participants in this study were from China, with
others coming from South Korea, Ecuador, Mongolia, Lebanon,
and Colombia (see Table 3.1). It should be noted that in this
chapter and throughout the book, I have rendered participants'
quotes in their own words, without correcting for standard
English usage. The only exception was small edits to remove
filler expressions such as *like*, as long as these did not change
the meaning being expressed.

Among the participants, the Chinese students appeared to
have the most similarity in their backgrounds and family structures, although their hometowns represented geographical, and
in some cases linguistic, diversity. For example, several participants spoke Mandarin, but one was a native speaker of Cantonese; some came from major cities in China, and others from
smaller towns. In terms of languages spoken, the East Asian
participants primarily spoke the language of their hometown
and studied English as a subject in school, whereas the non-
Asian participants tended to describe their experiences in more
multilingual terms; for example, the Middle Eastern participant
grew up speaking a mix of English and Arabic, and the Colombian participant spoke Spanish, French, and some English. All
participants were in their first year of study at a U.S. university,
but their previous educational contexts varied: Two participants
graduated from what they described as "traditional" public
high schools in their hometowns; two were transfer students

Table 3.1: List of Participants

Pseudonym	Age	Gender	Hometown	Language(s) Spoken in Home Environment	College	Major
Han Gil	18	Male	Chungju, South Korea	Korean	Business school	Marketing/ international business
Crystal	21	Female	Tianjin, China	Mandarin	Business school	Event management
Ai	19	Male	Guangzhou, China	Cantonese, Mandarin	Business school	Marketing/ international business
John	19	Male	Guayaquil, Ecuador	Spanish	Business school	Sports management
Amy	18	Female	Beijing, China	Mandarin	International affairs	International affairs
Lora	19	Female	Baotou, China (inner Mongolia)	Mandarin	Arts & sciences	Interior and architectural design
Michelle	22	Female	Ulan Bator, Mongolia	Mongolian	International affairs	International affairs
Kristen	18	Female	Beijing, China	Mandarin	Arts & sciences	Undecided (maybe public affairs)
Yoono	18	Male	Beirut, Lebanon	English & Arabic	Engineering	Civil engineering
Luca	19	Female	Bogota, Colombia	Spanish (French international school)	International affairs	International affairs (possible concentration in conflict resolution)

from universities in their home country; two spent the last two years of high school as exchange students in the United States; two graduated from an International Baccalaureate program within a school in their hometown; one went to a boarding school in India from the age of 12; and one attended a French international school from kindergarten, finishing out her high school education in a French international school in Bethesda, Maryland.

Family Influence

Despite this diversity, phenomenological research traditions aim to isolate that which is common across all participants—in other words, the essential elements of the experience being studied as a means of characterizing the phenomenon. In every case, participants described their context for mobility as being strongly influenced by their family. Participant responses revealed a common profile: a transnationally mobile student, whose experience was informed by access to global experiences, familial and financial support, and a fair amount of individual autonomy (see Table 3.2).

All participants described their parents as being educated and working, or having worked, in professional environments. While some participants' parents worked for a company or for the government, the majority had started their own businesses, and in the cases of Han Gil, John, and Luca, the business involved the entire family. In describing the role that family played in participants' ability to be transnationally mobile, it is also important to acknowledge that these opportunities are necessarily undergirded by a certain amount of financial security. Two participants, John and Yoono, described their families as being in the middle or upper class, while Lora described her family as "quite normal . . . not super rich or super poor." Few other participants mentioned their family's socio-economic status or the affordability of four years of study in the United States. Ai and Amy did mention that their opportunity to study abroad was facilitated by the financial situation of their families, and several participants described their parents as not having had the same opportunities to study or travel abroad in their youth, implying an upward mobility or an increase in global opportunities. In any case, it is safe to assume that an implicit element of each participant's experience was economic security.

Every participant also related some family connection to either studying or working abroad. In some cases, participants'

Table 3.2: Context for Mobility: Family Influence

Pseudonym (Country of Origin)	Parents' Profession (father; mother)	Representative Quotes on Family Role in Studying Abroad	International Experiences
Han Gil (South Korea)	Social work PhD;* Professor of social work (family-owned social work organization)	"My grandmother's friend's son studied there and he was kind of successful and the school is really well known in Asia, so, yeah, my parents decided to send me [to boarding school in India at age 12]."	Family travel to "a lot of Asian countries"
Crystal (China)	Chinese government employee; middle school teacher	Father's colleague had a daughter who transferred from a Chinese to U.S. university: "Then my father said, 'Oh, you can transfer too.' So I just transferred."	"I like travel but I don't have too much opportunity to travel"; some travel within China and one trip to SE Asia
Ai (China)	Owner of import-export business; former cosmetologist	"A few cousins, uh, they study abroad as well in Canada, in New Zealand, so our family is kind of all the children are going out somewhere study."	Family travel to Dubai, Singapore, and "a lot of different places"; two years as U.S. high school exchange student
John (Ecuador)	Family-owned shrimp business	"My dad have quite an interesting life. He was born in Ecuador but he moved to Italy like two years old and then he went to Germany when he was like 5 so he live in Germany until almost all his teenage years until he came back to Ecuador . . . he knows five languages."	Family traveled "quite a lot"; 17 school breaks in Miami
Amy (China)	"Boss" of news agency; sales manager in pharmaceutical company	"My father has many good friends, like foreign friends, and they come to my home and to talk . . . many of them diplomats like U.S. diplomats."	Family travel to Thailand, Europe, South Africa, United States; three trips to the United States for educational summer programs
Lora (China)	Manager of a steel company; medical doctor	"My parents have friend who live in U.S. and they are United States citizens and once we were having dinner and they inspired me to hear [about life abroad]."	Had not traveled abroad prior to studying in the United States but "father went to Mongolia because of business and my mother traveled with her friends to Europe."

Pseudonym (Country of Origin)	Parents' Profession (father; mother)	Representative Quotes on Family Role in Studying Abroad	International Experiences
Michelle (Mongolia)	Owner of frame company; accountant at mining company	"I have a brother who lived in the U.S. for five years . . . lived in DC" and he advised her to come.	Family travel to China, Russia; studied abroad in Japan
Kristen (China)	Investing company; investing company	"When I was born, my parents, they went to America for about 2 years so they have experience working here." (Parents left her with grandmother.)	Two years as U.S. high school exchange student
Yoono (Lebanon)	Family-owned business related to engineering*	"Both of my parents are Lebanese. I have lived in Lebanon my whole life, but my parents both studied in the States and they lived in the States for a while when they started working."	"I've actually traveled a lot." Family in NY and LA; traveled in United States, Europe, Australia
Luca (Colombia)	Owner of security consulting company; former owner of cake decorating business	Whole family moved to United States "for my education"	Family lived in Dominican Republic

*Parent completed degree in United States.
Note: Excerpts in the table are a combination of participants' direct speech, as indicated using quotation marks, and description paraphrased by the researcher.

relatives or family friends had studied abroad (Ai, Amy, Lora, Kristen), and in other cases, participants' parents themselves were educated in the United States or elsewhere overseas (Han Gil, Yoono, Michelle). For example, John said that he was "the first one of all [his] cousins to come out to study in the United States," but his father had extensive international experiences as he was growing up. The issue of mobility was further extended through participants' ability to travel with their families. All participants considered themselves to be generally well traveled; even if global travel had been limited, participants implied that their families were "open" to global opportunities. For example, though Crystal had few opportunities to travel because her father was so busy, her mother always told her "you need to go abroad to see." Among participants, there were also some cases of extreme global travel, for example Ai, Amy, Yoono, and John. John described himself as having "that blessing that I've been around the world quite a bit." Yoono indicated that his parents' education abroad, as well as his own travel, schooling, and access to the English language and U.S. culture, had a powerful influence on his perspective:

> I have lived in Lebanon my whole life, but my parents both studied in the States and they lived in the States for a while when they started working. And they moved back like a year before I was born, so I would say that definitely has an impact on the way I grew up, like the Western ideology, the mentality was a bit more open-minded. I have more of an open-minded mentality compared to some of the kids who I grew up with. So yeah, I feel that's one way my background shapes the way I am.

Yoono's explanation highlights not just his mobility, but the deep ways he felt his perspective had changed as a result of his family experiences overseas. These comments demonstrate that, for the ten participants, family experience abroad was a common theme across their lived experiences.

All participants were asked to describe the decision-making process to study abroad and noted the extent to which their families were involved. The idea of studying abroad was sometimes put forward by a parent or family member, as in the case of Han Gil, Crystal, Luca, Kristen, Michelle, and Yoono. Han Gil represented perhaps the most extreme case: His grandmother's friend's son had been "kind of successful" at a boarding school in India, so his family decided that he would go study there at the age of 12. Han Gil described not wanting to go at the beginning and having a difficult time transitioning to the boarding school: "I had homesick and I didn't know English at all. Like,

I couldn't even write my name, so for two or three years I had a really hard time getting used to the school." The rest of these participants remembered some hesitation when presented with the idea of studying abroad, but most seemed to agree with or accept the decision quite readily, with Yoono recalling: "I feel like [the idea to go to university in the United States] was first proposed by my parents, but I definitely agreed with them," and even Han Gil reflected back on being sent to school in India at age 12 and said "now I realize I made a correct choice to come to U.S. and go to India."

In almost half of the cases, however, participants emphasized that going to university in the United States was their own idea (Ai, John, Amy, Lora), which they then presented to their parents. Ai, for example, first proposed studying in the United States as a Chinese high school exchange student and spent two years at a Christian high school in a small town in Minnesota before enrolling in the university. Also, both Lora and John recalled having the idea to study abroad at a young age and telling their parents about it. John related his father's response in these terms: "When I was real little I had this idea, I think when I was like 14 years old, I told my dad like that, you know, when I grow up, I am going to go out, and he was like, yeah, you should, with those grades and your determination, you have to go out." Lora's and Amy's fathers were in immediate support of the idea while their mothers initially preferred that they study closer to home; as Lora said, "At first my mother was kind of disappointed because she doesn't want me to leave her, and my father was kind of approved my decisions and he wants me to get better education and experience more and feel the world and explore the world and something like that. He thinks it's better for me to go out and see." Amy said that her family was lucky enough to be able to afford to send her, so she thought, "I have this chance. I'm gonna go grab it." Regardless of who initiated the idea of study abroad, families were involved in the decision, and participants described their relationships with their families as supportive and close.

Once the family decision to study abroad was made, participants perceived having relative autonomy in moving the decision forward, often taking it upon themselves to prepare for the TOEFL® and SAT®, research universities, and untangle application procedures. All participants demonstrated an awareness of which U.S. colleges and universities were the "best" to attend, and several participants spent their summer breaks touring U.S. college campuses, applying to ten or more different schools—many of them relatively prestigious private universities in the eastern United States. Comments demonstrated a surprising comparative awareness of U.S. schools: "I actually had [considered] many other competitive high-ranking—yeah, that's kind of a lot of [what we] Chinese students think about and our parents . . . [and] then I apply to a lot of high-ranking schools" (Ai); "I look at a book, like the best, the top best 100 universities in the world, and oh, Toronto University—this one is so beautiful. I just look at the picture, and I say this one is beautiful, but then I think, like, because you look at the whole education, Canada is not as good as America, so I just came here" (Crystal); "I feel like the students like study here like in a famous university. It's easier to get job in China . . . I applied to like 15 different universities" (Kristen); "I knew that engineering was definitely the thing I wanted to study, like it's a degree that I felt that, one, I would most likely succeed in because I have more of a technical mind and, two, it was something I had a decent passion for compared to other degrees. And so I applied to many notable schools that offer engineering" (Yoono). This strategic awareness implies that participants were not limited in their set of options and also sets the stage for the theme described later: motivation to study abroad based on perceived opportunity.

Opportunity versus Pressure

When asked to describe their motivation for attending college in the United States, opportunity was the overwhelming theme among responses, with little indication that a sense of pressure accompanied the decision. Sometimes this opportunity was conceived of as practical—that is, how an education abroad would improve their future prospects or ability to pursue the job of their choice. The following quotes illustrate how participants perceived higher education abroad as an opportunity to improve their English, study a particular major, or have access to jobs:

- "Because in Mongolia, if we graduate from abroad university or something like that, it is much easier to get a job and so that world is more globalizing and that we need, like, a second language or a third language." (Michelle, on motivation for transferring from a Mongolian university)
- "I don't want to continue social work [his family business] because all they do is basically donate. We earn almost nothing out of it. And then I know even though we have a lot of cash, I know it is going to run out in a very short time, so it is better for me to choose a major which can earn money rather than spend." (Han Gil, on why he chose to do a business degree in the United States)
- "I would like to [work for my family business], but I think I more likely to start my own company [in sports management]. That's my dream. I don't know—I want to start for myself. I really idolize—I love my grandpa because he started, kind of, from the bottom but literally he just went to third grade and stopped there and he build all the empire from that." (John, on the prospect of working for his family's shrimp business)
- "I want more useful education but not just random college, so I heard that United States' college is the best in the world so that make me decide to come here." (Lora, on why she did not want to go to college in China)
- "First of all, I feel the style of education is better in the States, and in Lebanon there was this one university, the American University of Beirut, which was the school that everybody went to, like, after graduating from high school—most of the kids who wanted to stay in Lebanon decided to go and all went to that school 'cause it was the most prestiged. And it was most recognized by other countries, but the thing is the school was actually right

next to my house. Life would have just been the same way
it was before." (Yoono, on why he did not want to attend
the American University in Beirut)

When reflecting on the decision to study abroad, there was
surprisingly little discussion of participants being motivated
to have American friends or integrate into American society,
although Lora mentioned her excitement at wanting to know
what "Americans are really like," and Amy described a turning
point in her life when, at age 15, she was asked by her father
to act as a tour guide for a college student visiting China from
the United States. Not only did she feel like it was her first
time being "a really independent person," but it helped solidify
Amy's decision to come to the United States to study, to "go to
another place on my own and then try to see how, what, things
I can do on my own." This hints at a far more prevalent motivation that participants conveyed: self-actualization and moving
beyond the borders of their previous lives. Comments that represented this theme include: "My mom wanted me to see more
of the world not just study in China" (Crystal); "I just feel like I
am missing something . . . go out and see the world—what's the
world like" (Ai); "I feel like many kids who stay are like—they
are afraid to take a challenge. They just want to stay with their
parents and live the good life, but I feel like once you are 18,
you have to learn to live on your own" (Yoono); "My vision was
really small [but I wanted to] learn English and go to a bigger
country to learn more" (Han Gil).

Additionally, John described the process of feeling torn
between his comfortable home life, surrounded by his friends
and a supportive family, and wanting to be independent and to
challenge himself:

They [his parents] had, like, idea that they would send
me here to be independent, to grow myself and to do
my things. 'Cause the thing is, every time I need to do a
paperwork or something, my mom just fill the things. . . .
So here everything I'm by my own so that's, like, kind of

the challenge they wanted to give me when I was going out. I wanted that deep inside me, but I was actually pretty comfortable, like, my parents doing everything for me so I was just, kind of, a collage between what I want and what I need.

John's comment implies that he was comfortable at home with his family and friends—a sentiment other participants admitted having—and that, though he wanted to be independent and "go out," it was also tempting to stay in his protected home environment.

Perception of Leaving a Constrained System

For participants, the motivation of opportunity was juxtaposed with limitations they perceived in their home country. In particular, participants characterized higher educational opportunities at home as being constrained or inadequate. Ai emphasized that China has a "huge population" and that going abroad "is probably a good choice to make yourself a little bit different." Amy noted that "[in China] the entrance exam is only once a year so students only have one chance to prove themselves and it's really, really competitive, so my school—most of the students decide to enter a Chinese university. So they work really, really hard to try to prove themselves and do well in that exam." When Chinese students matriculate in a university, however, Kristen— who decided to apply to U.S. universities after having "gotten used" to American education during two years as a high school exchange student—noted that at "some universities in China . . . the students don't have to study very hard, they just want to get pass the course [with] like 60 points and they didn't use the time in the university like as well as students here." Lora described college in China as being more like "kindergarten." For Crystal, because her hometown university did not have a strong program in her field, she thought her chance of getting into a good U.S. graduate school for marketing would be nearly impossible if she graduated from a domestically based program, so she transferred from a local university to a U.S. one.

Participants from outside of China also discussed constraints within their home environment as a motivation to attend university abroad. Han Gil, who came from a province in the central region of Korea, said, "If you go to university near my city, like, they would be ranked, like, 20, 30 in Korea, which is really low. Then I will not even get a proper job . . . because honestly in Korea, if you don't have a higher education, it is impossible to get a job." In John's case, he said: "My mom actually supported [the decision to study abroad] because she says, Ecuador in a higher education system is not that good . . . you should go outside and all your brothers should go so you have to focus on other stuff." Luca's family had moved to the Dominican Republic when she was young, but when it came to higher education, neither of her previous schooling environments were seen as desirable: "Um, the Dominican Republic, it's an island, it's not—it really doesn't have really good universities. And the academics are not good. So it was either [that or] go back to Colombia, which was not an option," due to her family circumstances. Though there was a prestigious American university in his hometown that many of his peers attended, Yoono recalled a conversation in which his father, who had completed his undergraduate education there, told him: "I would feel for you it is much better if you study abroad [rather than at the American University of Beirut]."

Overall, statements about participants' motivation to study abroad demonstrated that their decision to go to a U.S. university was influenced both by family background and by some perception of an opportunity to be gained by studying abroad; in no case did a participant convey the decision to pursue higher education abroad or to study a particular subject or work in a particular field as "pressure." Even Han Gil, whose parents sent him abroad against his will at 12, recalled how his family perceived the relationship between studying abroad and his future life: "They always tell me it is your choice—your life is your choice. My father always tell me I will help you to your study but later on is all your life so you have to earn money and do whatever you want to do."

Participants described leaving their families with a combination of anxiety and excitement. Some had the extended benefit of a family presence even in the United States, such as Luca, whose family moved to Maryland in large part so that the children could go to school there, and Michelle, who was so unhappy after three days in the dormitory that her mother and brother came to live with her in a suburban Virginia apartment. Others were able to fly to the United States for college accompanied by family; for example, Lora's parents and John's mother and godmother traveled with them to help them get settled in. Amy, who flew to orientation alone, described her departure as being:

> ... full of like joy and tears. Tears from my mom and me ... I was pretty nervous before that departure for like a few days. I was really, really anxious because I—well, I have to say my English was not that good. I cannot express what I read—I cannot always express what I really want to say and or correctly, but so I am wondering whether I can find real friends here, like can I fit in? ... but then on that departure day I also felt a little bit proud because I am really finally achieve my goal, and finally I am really going to live alone by myself or without my parents' help and probably without any other friend's help because I don't know anyone before I come here.

Kristen, who arrived in rural Iowa as a high school sophomore, made three flight connections on her own to get there, all the while feeling this way:

> I really have no idea about the life here and, um, I don't know how my English skill is but I just flew here with just "I don't know nothing," and I come here. I was exciting and luckily my host family, they're really nice.

Ai, who also studied as an exchange student, described flying out of China with this feeling:

> I still remember that moment when I left airport and I cry and my mom and dad are teary-eyed and we miss each other and I turn my face down because they are crying. I cannot see their face again because I am going to cry again, so I leave briefly and then I walk into the security point and then, okay, that's my journey begins. That's my new page of my life.

Regardless of the level of autonomy these students demonstrated, or the security and support they had from their families, they were all undertaking a new experience that required a fair amount of courage.

4

Classrooms as Socio-Academic Spaces

Chapters 2 and 3 introduced the broader context that frames this study and offered a brief introduction of the participants whose voices and stories fill this book. This chapter takes a step back to situate this project in its research context, including its deep philosophical and methodological heritage, the socio-academic space model it engendered, and the study's research design. The chapters that then follow will illuminate the lived experience of the study's participants at three points in time during the semester they were taking the theme-based FYW course at a U.S. university.

Underlying Qualitative Traditions

Qualitative research can be a powerful tool in helping us understand educational contexts, practices, and experiences. Creswell (2007) indicated that qualitative research constitutes the "study of research problems inquiring into the meaning individuals or groups ascribe to social or human problems" (p. 37). Qualitative inquiry is known to be situational, often taking place in a natural setting or linked to an actual experience. Other overarching features of qualitative approaches include the researcher's role as a key instrument, the use multiple sources of data, inductive data analysis, a focus on participants' meanings, an emergent design, and a theoretical/contextual framework—all resulting in a holistic account of a complex situation or problem (Creswell,

2007; Merriam, 2009). The problems investigated in qualitative research are not necessarily easily addressed by quantitative research, but are still systematically investigated and analyzed; such problems "span the social and human sciences" and are often deeply involved in "issues of gender, culture, and marginalized groups" (Creswell, 2007, p. 43). A key reason for conducting qualitative research is to find a "complex, detailed understanding of an issue" that comes directly from the source and is imbued with contextual awareness. In order to "empower individuals to share their stories, hear their voices, and minimize the power relationships that often exist between the researcher and participants in the field" (Creswell, 2007, p. 40), a climate of mutual respect and collaboration should be established among all members of the research endeavor.

Inherent in qualitative designs is a series of thoughtful philosophical considerations. Researchers position themselves in relation to certain philosophical assumptions, which range from epistemological and ontological concerns to methodological and rhetorical arrangements, and these in turn drive the design of the study. Along these lines, in qualitative research of this type, reality is treated as "multiple and subjective" and captured through the voice of the participants. The researcher is tightly linked with participants, and the values and biases of both tend to be implicated in the research. In addition, the research design is likely to be inductive and emergent, and personal voice and an expressive literary style are rhetorical features of the writing (Creswell, 2007, p. 17). Given these dimensions of the qualitative tradition, it was clear to me that a qualitative approach, using a hermeneutic phenomenological methodology, was the proper path for this particular inquiry. Broadly speaking, such an approach aims to understand one's lifeworld, gaining a "deeper understanding of the nature and meaning" of everyday experiences (van Manen, 1990, p. 9).

Epistemology and Worldview

Epistemology represents an underlying theory of knowledge that guides our understanding of the world as well as our research practices (Creswell, 2007; Crotty, 1998; Schwandt, 2000; Wiersma & Jurs, 2005). This particular research was broadly considered constructivist, an epistemological position that has been linked to hermeneutic methodologies (Lincoln & Guba, 2000). An over-arching definition of constructivism/constructionism has been offered by Crotty (1998): "The view that all knowledge, and there-fore all meaningful reality as such, is contingent upon human practices, being constructed in and out of interaction between human beings and their world, and developed and transmitted within an essentially social context" (p. 42). When individuals cross boundaries and engage in a shared socio-academic experi-ence, such as a first-year writing class, they operate in interaction with one another, their setting, and their individual understand-ings and experiences. In addition, the core of this inquiry was grounded in an understanding of knowledge as it "refers us back to our world, our lives, to who we are, and to what makes us read, write, and talk together as educators: it is what stands iconically behind the words, the speaking and the language" (van Manen, 1990, p. 46). In other words, through this research, I conceived of this phenomenon as being experienced in relation to both the worlds of my participants and that of myself as a researcher and educator.

The worldview that framed this inquiry was social construc-tionism, which is driven by an acknowledgement that meanings can be "varied and multiple" (Creswell, 2007, p. 20). As a result, there is a powerful need to hear and understand participants' viewpoints. The meanings participants derive are often "nego-tiated socially and historically . . . formed through interactions with others and through historical and cultural norms that operate in individuals' lives" (p. 21). A social constructionist per-spective has powerful links to the writing classroom because it emphasizes the role of language and power relationships in set-tings where social, cultural, and academic knowledge is negoti-ated (Kennedy, 2006). Given the nature of the phenomenon I was studying and the background knowledge and experiences of my participants, this perspective was extremely relevant. I also saw this worldview as appropriate for this research because it animated both policy and praxis, demonstrating that particular institutional decisions should not be separated from the reality of the experience for individuals in that setting. In this case, both the histories of L2 writers in these mainstream classrooms and their day-to-day experiences in this particular setting shaped their understanding of what it *meant* to live that experience.

Origins of Phenomenology

Phenomenology begins with a human experience, some type of phenomenon, to be investigated and better understood. At its root, *phenomenology* is based on a philosophical premise and intends to develop a "composite description of the essence of the experience for all of the individuals" (Creswell, 2007, p. 58). While phenomenology is driven by an understanding of lived experience, it is intertwined with a consciousness that represents human beings' interaction with the world in which they live. In other words, keying into a phenomenon depends on an awareness of the reality we are living through and our ability to retrospectively engage with the experience (van Manen, 1990). Phenomenology seeks to articulate the essence of a particular lived experience, hence universalizing its structural characteristics. van Manen (1990) calls this a "systematic attempt to uncover and describe the structures, the internal meaning structures, of lived experience" so as to understand the phenomenon with greater depth (p. 10).

Edmund Husserl is often associated with the idea of phenomenology as a mode of inquiry. Though initially a mathematician, Husserl transitioned into the field of philosophy, and his move toward phenomenology stemmed in part from his critique of psychology's attempt to examine human experiences using methods from the natural sciences. Husserl believed that individuals and the lifeworld they experience are not separable, and that by looking at everyday phenomena intentionally, we can potentially "uncover new and/or forgotten meanings" and "reach true meaning through penetrating deeper and deeper into reality" (Laverty, 2003, pp. 22–23). The core concepts of intentionality and essences underpinned Husserl's phenomenological approach, and the process of discovering these essences was characterized by the researcher "bracketing" his or her own beliefs and assumptions about the phenomenon. In other words, the researcher would suspend judgment in order to focus on the actual experience—the "thing itself"—and how it is understood by those who live through it (Laverty, 2003; van Manen, 1990). Methodologically, phenomenological research results in a careful description of the underlying structure of a particular experience, without the influence of any interpretive judgments.

Hermeneutic Phenomenology

Though there are several branches of research associated with phenomenology, this study drew on a *hermeneutic* approach, which according to van Manen (1990) is considered the "theory and practice of interpretation," named for the Greek god Hermes, who is said to have transmitted messages from gods to humans (p. 179). Hermeneutic interpretive practices were historically applied to religious texts with the goal of understanding that which may appear obscure (Nakkula & Ravitch, 1998; van Manen, 1990). Rather than a purely phenomenological treatment, one that intended to structurally isolate and describe the essential features of this experience, this research occupied the space between phenomenology and hermeneutics. I wanted to know the shape underlying the experience of these L2 writers in mainstream composition classrooms, but at the same time I wanted to know how my participants came to understand this experience, the meaning they made of it, throughout the process of living it. In this sense, a hermeneutic approach allowed me to draw more on interpretation than on pure description, focusing on the "historical meanings of experience and their developmental effects on individual and social levels" (Laverty, 2003, p. 27). In educational settings, such an attentiveness to experience, as shaped by broader social contexts, enables stronger connections between theory and practice to be established.

It is generally acknowledged that Wilhelm Dilthey, a 19th century German historian, and Martin Heidegger, originally a German theologian who was trained in phenomenological practices by Husserl, were pivotal actors in the hermeneutic shift in the study of lived phenomena (Nakkula & Ravitch, 1998; Ricoeur, 1981; van Manen, 1990). Dilthey's core concern was the source of historical knowledge. The human sciences, Dilthey claimed, assume that individuals have the capacity to "transpose [themselves] into the mental lives of others" (Ricoeur, 1981, p. 49). Human understanding was thus characterized by interconnectivity, and hermeneutics enabled individuals to connect themselves to universal aspects of human history (Ricoeur, 1981). Therefore, the capacity to understand the lived experience of culturally, historically, and socially situated individuals is not only associated with the text itself but also with the text as projected *into* the wider world. To frame this idea more specifically, we need to understand French philosopher Paul Ricoeur's (1981) notion of the relationship between discourse and text. He considered discourse part of an "internal dialectic between event and meaning" (p. 11) that is associated with a happening that is ephemeral in nature. Text is an extension of this discourse based on a "distanciation," or a decontextualized rendering of the spoken discourse in written form. In hermeneutic traditions, this text—as a realization of discourse—becomes the site of interpretive activity.

Heidegger's initial approach to the study of lived experience was grounded in an ontological perspective: At its core was the question of *being*, which Heidegger characterizes as *Dasein*, or the source from which the notion of "being" is questioned (Ricoeur, 1981; van Manen, 1990). An understanding of the world can only arise based on a conceptualization of being-in-the-world; Ricoeur elaborated this point by saying that we must "find ourselves *there* and *feel* ourselves even before we orientate ourselves" (1981, p. 56). Heidegger considered discourse to be the manner of articulating the understanding that emerges from our fundamental sense of being-in-the-world, and we are naturally tied to a pre-understanding that cannot be separated from our historical, social, and cultural roots (Laverty, 2003).

This study looked at L2 international students with strong cultural, linguistic, and personal identities who had been put in a setting that may have varied greatly from their previous experiences—in other words, their roots. In addition, the nature of the phenomenon under study aligned very well with Heidegger's hermeneutic notion of "thrownness" (Nakkula & Ravitch, 1998, p. 5). Into every new experience, we are *thrown* from our histories, including our cultures, societies, families, all manner of our experiences, and how we have made sense of everything that has come before.

Hans-Georg Gadamer, a 20th century French philosopher, advanced this notion in his hermeneutic consideration of the arcs of projection and reflection. The *projection arc* is when we are *within* the actual experience, the "movement into and engagement with actions," and the *reflection arc* is when we make sense of the experience we have been projected into (Nakkula & Ravitch, 1998, p. 25). According to Gadamer, language is the primary means through which we develop and articulate our understanding. Thus, our engagement with the arcs of projection and reflection can be both empowered and restrained by language. In fact, in relying on the "voice" of the participant to convey lived experience, the importance of language cannot be overemphasized. van Manen (1990) drew on Heidegger and Ricoeur in developing his point that "lived experience is soaked through with language" (p. 38). He further advised the researcher to pay attention to participants' everyday use of language, which is rich with clues about the experience and their interpretation of it; in this regard, one should "reflectively hold on to the verbal manifestations that appear to possess interpretive significance for the actual phenomenological description" (p. 62). The narrative text that is derived from participants' rendering of the experience, as well as the gestures and silences that accompany it, becomes a rich source of analysis.

A second key consideration of Gadamer's was that because understanding and interpretation are so tightly bound, we are constantly positioned within any research on human experiences; in other words, our consciousness is so deeply ingrained that we cannot objectively and definitively characterize a phenomenon or detach ourselves fully from the matter that we study (Laverty, 2003; Ricoeur, 1981; Schwandt, 2000). As van Manen (1990), drawing on Gadamer, stated, "The reader belongs to the text that he or she is reading" (p. 180). That is to say, we explore the meaning of a lived experience by seeking to understand the "local and specifically constructed" (p. 180) reality of individuals, with full knowledge that as researchers and readers, we have beliefs, experiences, and assumptions that shape our own interaction with the material. This contention dovetails neatly with the social constructionist approach, in which the researcher and participants engage in a shared and situated research experience.

Van Manen's Approach to Researching Lived Experience

Because my research was pedagogically grounded, I sought an approach to hermeneutic phenomenology that both aligned with the philosophical lineage outlined above and with my intent as a situated researcher to produce a culturally sensitive and reflective written text. Thus I turned to Max van Manen's (1990) action sensitive pedagogic approach for this study. In many ways, van Manen's approach conflates phenomenology and hermeneutics by offering a mutually reinforcing combination of phenomenology's description (as captured in the facts of the lived experience) and hermeneutics' interpretation (as captured in the meaning as conveyed through language).

Van Manen (1990) identified six key features of hermeneutic phenomenological research that need to be in a "dynamic interplay" for any human science inquiry with pedagogic intent. First, the phenomenon we study must be of enduring interest to us and "commit us to the world." Second, we must explore the phenomenon as it is lived, rather than as it is conceptualized. Third, we must isolate the essential characteristics of the experience through reflection, and fourth, recursively "write our way to a description of that phenomenon." Fifth, we should not pretend to be disinterested in the experience under study and instead must orient ourselves strongly to that which we study. Finally, this approach needs to be based on a constant conceptual movement between the parts and the whole, fine-tuning our understanding of the lived experience (pp. 30–34). The commitment evident in these six features ran through my own data collection, analysis, interpretation, and representation.

Subjectivity: The Researcher in the Research

One of the benefits of a hermeneutic phenomenological approach was that, as a researcher, I did not have to "bracket out" my subjectivity. van Manen's (1990) action sensitive approach includes a notion of subjectivity that derives from a strong personal orientation to the object of study and an awareness of any embedded assumptions; the researcher should remain "perceptive, insightful, and discerning," which enables the full meaning of the experience to be better revealed (p. 20). It was important for me to lay bare my subjectivity in this project because the better part of my career has been spent educating L2 writers in U.S. institutional settings. As a result of my experience, including readings of scholarly literature and interactions with others in institutional settings, I have come to find that some L2 students feel marginalized in mainstream college composition classes, and that without intending to, L1 students and instructors may create an environment that isolates those who are outside of the linguistic and cultural mainstream. Though Merriam (2009) argued that, in qualitative research, the researcher acts as a "primary instrument" for data collection and analysis (p. 15), as a *human* instrument I had to be careful to reveal my stake in the research, including any assumptions or experiences that may have influenced the study. Because of my background and disposition as it related to the challenges L2 writers may have in mainstream classrooms, I needed to be aware of how my biases and subjectivities "may [have been] shaping the collection and interpretation of my data" (Merriam, 2009, p. 15). For example, I may have extended my anecdotal experiences with students' anxiety about taking that class to a general assumption that L2 students may feel overwhelmed by the cultural content of the FYW class.

Sociocultural Theoretical Influences

My framing of the FYW classroom as the site for this project also reflects key characteristics of sociocultural theory, which is often associated with Russian psychologist Lev Vygotsky and premised on the assumption that meaning is "culturally and historically situated" and "constructed, reconstructed, and transformed" through mediated social interactions (Englert, Mariage, & Dunsmore, 2006, p. 208). Vygotsky's key contribution to constructivist theory was his contention that such development is *transactive*, whereby increased understanding is generated in social settings and supported by interactions with more experienced peers or adults. This construction of knowledge takes place in what Vygotsky calls the Zone of Proximal Development (ZPD), a space where new knowledge can be made intelligible through active engagement with the material in the ZPD setting. This is a notion that links neatly to teaching and learning in institutional settings (Kennedy, 2006; Kozulin et al., 2003; Lantolf & Poehner, 2008; MacArthur, Graham, & Fitzgerald, 2006).

Another link between sociocultural theory and the FYW classroom experience I explore stems from the notion that "activity is situated in concrete interactions that are simultaneously improvised locally and mediated by prefabricated, historically provided tools and practices" and involves external representations, such as speech or writing, collaboration with others within the setting, and internalized learning and meaning making (MacArthur, Graham, & Fitzgerald, 2006, p. 55). Sociocultural theory is often invoked in relation to writing and the college writing classroom, which serves as a site of enculturation for students into a higher-level academic discourse community. Participation in a writing classroom can be considered a situated activity that links the cultural and historical with pragmatic production, which in turn helps to explain "how culture comes to be embodied in practice" (p. 64). When we look at culturally and linguistically diverse writing classrooms, or even a classroom that includes a single L2 student, we must further contend with the influence of context, culture, and pedagogical approaches on student experiences.

The experiences of L2 students in mainstream settings are further mediated by the process of language acquisition, whereby the acquisition and use of a second language is internalized through interactions in the language-learning setting

(Lantolf & Pavlenko, 1995; Lantolf & Poehner, 2008). In line with Vygotsky's thinking, language acquisition is developed through the interaction of the cognitive domain—our brain's capacity for language learning—and the external, or social, domain that mediates our construction of meaning. The application of sociocultural theory is fairly common in composition studies (Englert, Mariage, & Dunsmore; 2006; Kennedy, 2006; MacArthur, Graham, & Fitzgerald, 2006; Prior, 2006), as well as in research on L2 writing (Atkinson, 2002; Cumming, 1998; Donato & McCormick, 1994; Leki, Cumming, & Silva, 2008; Zuengler & Miller, 2006).

According to a research synthesis by Leki, Cumming, and Silva (2008), considerable work in the field has interpreted instructional practices and classroom interactions through Vygotsky's Zone of Proximal Development, including the role of tutors, instructor interaction and feedback, and student reflective analysis in L2 writing. The research of Donato and McCormick (1994) examined how L2 learning was mediated through classroom culture, a point that had particular salience for my study of L2 writers' experience in a mainstream composition class. The authors also noted that the classroom represents a sort of sociocultural activity system in which "collaborative interaction, intersubjectivity, and assisted performance occur" (p. 455). As such, activity theory, which was strongly influenced by Vygotskyian thinking, also served to conceptually shape my study. The FYW classroom was a good example of a situated activity system because its participants were engaged in activities that had a specific direction or end goal.

The notion of classroom learning as contextually driven and situated was highly relevant to my research approach. Situated learning, as a theoretical proposition, is highly contextualized and relational, and meanings are derived through negotiated interactions in specific contexts (Watson-Gegeo, 2004; Zuengler & Miller, 2006). The epistemologies that underlie these contextual interactions are often the result of broader sociohistorical processes and developments, and the consideration of these factors is germane to any study of L2 writers' experiences in mainstream classrooms. Perhaps the most frequently cited treatment of situated learning comes from Lave and Wenger (1991), who popularized the terms *communities of practice* and *legitimate peripheral participation*. Socialization into a particular socio-academic community, for instance, is characterized by a kind of apprenticeship relationship. As Zuengler and Miller (2006) noted, situated learning "foregrounds learners' participation in particular social practices, understood as habitual ways people (re)produce material and symbolic resources, often attached to particular times and places, and comprising communities of practice in complex, often overlapping ways" (p. 41). For the purposes of this study, it was interesting to note the extent to which the focus on L2 writers' classroom experience over time—in other words, through a series of interviews over the course of the semester—demonstrated growth from limited participation to fuller participation in the mainstream composition "community of practice."

The Socio-Academic Space Model

As noted previously, this research conceived of a mainstream writing classroom as a socio-academic space, a shared environment where course content and formal academic tasks are combined with mediated social interactions among members of the classroom community (instructor and students), all of whom carry with them unique sociocultural histories and perspectives. Meanings are derived through negotiated interactions in this specific context (Watson-Gegeo, 2004; Zuengler & Miller, 2006). Thus, instead of an approach that focused primarily on the acquisition of skills or knowledge in a classroom setting, I considered the classroom a socially constructed "space" in which participant experiences were shaped by their socio-cultural histories and self-understandings, the practical realities and tasks of the course—including the underlying assumptions, ideologies, and knowledge bases—and their attitudes about and interactions with others.

Figure 4.1: Socio-Academic Space in Educational Settings

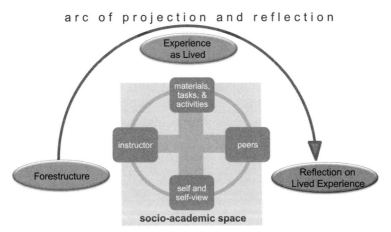

This framework in Figure 4.1 offers a new perspective on the relational and transactive aspects of meaning making in educational settings. Experiences in socio-academic settings, though to some extent "controlled" phenomena (in time and circumstance), are nonetheless part of a broader lived arc of understanding. Meaning is created through experiences as they are interpreted and made sense of. In turn, these experiences set the infrastructure—or schema—that allows our brains to interpret future experiences. Particularly relevant to this study was the notion that this process of development is tightly linked with an individual's previous socio-historical experiences; in other words, meaning is actively derived from the interrelationship among elements of an individual's social, cultural, and cognitive landscapes.

Research Design in Line with the Socio-Academic Space Model

The study I conducted was designed to elucidate the lived experience of L2 students in a mainstream first-year writing course at an urban, private U.S. research university through a hermeneutic phenomenological investigation of two main research questions: *Within a framework of the internationalization of higher*

*education, how do L2 international students experience and under-
stand being part of a required mainstream first-year writing course at a
private U.S. university? To what extent does the thematic nature of the
course mediate the students' experience?*

As a researcher, my goal was to have a thoughtful and contextually grounded methodological approach to my research
questions, guided by the nature of the experience under study,
as well as its "personal, institutional, and substantive" elements
(van Manen, 1990, p. 163). Data needed to be collected in a natural environment and with a high level of sensitivity toward
both the participants and the setting (Crotty, 1998). The site for
this study was a university in the eastern United States with a
first-year (mainstream) writing requirement that applied to all
students who matriculated there, meaning that even the L2 students who initially complete sheltered EAP coursework in academic writing were required to complete the first-year writing
course successfully, which, in essence, mandates inclusion.

The experience of L2 writers was more specifically located
in an academic writing course designed to enable first-year university students to develop skills and techniques for academic
writing through access to intellectually stimulating thematic
course content in a small-group seminar format. Despite a uniform template of course objectives, each instructor had a unique
approach and tailored his or her course to a particular intellectual theme that is considered relevant or of interest to first-year
writers within the academic discourse community. Therefore, a
unique feature of this study was that participants were engaged
in the same overall experience—that of a topically oriented
mainstream writing class—but did not necessarily share the
same theme or classroom experience. This helped ensure broad
coverage of the phenomenon and bring in diverse voices and
perspectives. My aim was to engage in meaningful conversation
with L2 writers who were experiencing the phenomenon and
had an insider perspective and a willingness to share.

In line with this goal, I employed criterion sampling for this
study, ensuring that all participants fit the same criteria for inclusion: international undergraduates from non–English speaking

backgrounds who had matriculated at the university and were enrolled in the mainstream first-year writing class—in other words, those who were directly experiencing the phenomenon and could contribute to a better understanding of it (Creswell, 2007). I sought "information-rich cases" in order to gain insights into this particular lived experience (Merriam, 2009, p. 77). After securing Institutional Review Board (IRB) approval, I invited the participation of all L2 students who had taken an EAP writing course in the previous semester and who were currently enrolled in the first-year writing class. In the end, 10 participants who were experiencing the phenomenon completed all three interviews and served as data sources for this study.

Because my qualitative study was "anchored in a real-life situation," I hoped to be able to gather sufficient data to present a "rich, holistic account" (Merriam, 2009, p. 51) of the lived experiences of my participants in a thematically oriented mainstream college writing class. This methodology emphasized the hermeneutic significance of the phenomenon, where understandings were awakened through reflection and articulation in a conversational setting (van Manen, 1990). According to Merriam (2009), interviews are considered the primary means to access the "underlying structure of the meaning of the experience" (p. 25), which is the main task of phenomenological research. Engaging in semi-structured interviews made it possible to have a purposeful conversation with my participants, paying attention to how they made meaning of the situation—in other words, their social construction—and trying to see the experience from their perspective (Merriam, 2009). Capturing the "voice" of my participants through these interviews further enabled me to add dimension and depth to my description of the lived experience. I wanted my data sources to contribute to the reliability and robustness of my findings and to offer a "thick description" of the interaction of classroom variables over time (Merriam, 2009, p. 43).

The data collection took place over the course of an academic semester, allowing me to capture the scope of the experience because over time "classroom practices and social structures are mutually constitutive in shaping students' identity and achievement" (Chiang & Schmida, 2006, p. 106). Three interviews were conducted with each participant during the semester in which they were enrolled in the course in order to capture the "arc" of participants' experiences over time, in line with the socio-academic space model. The semi-structured, relatively open-ended interview format generated some very rich data while not losing sight of the phenomenon itself. It is important to emphasize that the interview was not a loose conversation but rather one that was fundamentally grounded in the purpose of the research, staying as close as possible to the actual experience under study (van Manen, 1990). I drew on Patton's (2002) guidelines for effective qualitative interviews, directing my questions to participants' (a) experience and behavior; (b) opinion and values; (c) affective responses; (d) knowledge; (e) senses; and (f) background/demographic data. I conducted multiple interviews over time to tap into the cumulative experience of each participant, drawing upon the systematic approach established by Seidman (1998), which begins with a focused life history, continues with the details of the experience, and concludes with a reflection on the meaning of the experience.

During and immediately after the interviews, researcher-written memos were generated as part of the "ongoing interpretive activity" of hermeneutic inquiry (Nakkula & Ravitch, 1998, p. 48). In terms of data analysis for this study, a coding structure was developed based on emergent themes that were identified in the data and in supporting memos, eventually resulting in a coding scheme that aligned with the purpose of the study. The approach to isolating themes for data analysis was based on van Manen's (1990) selective or highlighting method, which identifies meaningful phrases that capture the experience. This process begins with a type of open coding, whereby texts are read with an eye to phrases or ideas that illuminated the experience and can be categorized and labeled as codes. This process is somewhat expansive in the early stages, but eventually codes are narrowed and focused into a tentative framework for findings, and data is culled anew to align with this coding structure (Merriam, 2009).

In the next three chapters, the findings that were inductively rendered from this analysis have been organized across time and theme so as to capture the "arc" of this phenomenon in the experiences of these participants. Whenever possible, unedited direct quotes are used to capture the voices of these ten students, who helped construct and reveal their experience in this socio-academic space.

5

Entering the First-Year Writing Course:
Hopeful but Unsure

A key motivation for this project was to understand better how L2 students, who choose to study in the United States, experience "mainstream" curricular requirements such as first-year writing. Thus, the timing of the first set of participant interviews was deliberately arranged to coincide with their entry point into this new academic setting to capture the sensation of the students' being "thrown" into this new situation.

Early questions during the first interview explored participants' histories and decisions to study abroad, in the context of their responses to questions about previous experiences with writing in school, as discussed in Chapter 2. The first interview went on to explore their selection of the section of the FYW class, their understanding of the course theme, and their initial impressions and expectations. Key themes that cut across the experience of participants as they entered this new socio-academic space were: (1) writing as an unfamiliar "required" subject in their home country's educational context; (2) course selection, which revealed that the course theme mattered; (3) perception of self in this particular socio-academic space.

Writing as an Unfamiliar "Required" Subject

Though all participants had taken an EAP academic writing course the semester before taking FYW, I was interested in

Figure 5.1: Entering the Socio-Academic Space

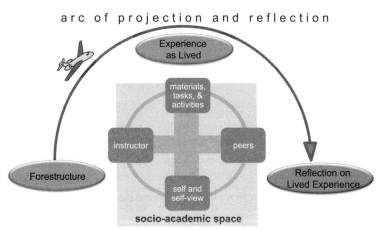

understanding their experiences with writing in their home country educational context. One particularly salient finding of this study was that the writing or composition class as we know it was absent from the previous experiences of the participants. Though writing was a core skill in their academic experiences, participants indicated that a class such as this did not exist in any of their previous educational settings. They also noted the absence of a single topical theme for the writing that they did in schooling in their home country, which reinforced the unfamiliarity they may have felt when coming into a FYW course that was thematic in nature. Participants educated in U.S.-based settings or international schools abroad made mention of literature courses that required writing essays and/or research papers, however. For example, Ai, Kristen, and Han Gil mentioned taking English literature courses in high school but not having a particular course dedicated to writing. John and Yoono, who both graduated from International Baccalaureate (IB) programs in their home country, also agreed that no single course for writing existed; as John said, "There was no, like, writing course. So basically, like, in the English class the writing part was included, so and it was, like, the main focus. So I think there is where I learned all my writing and stuff." Luca, who attended a French international school, also said that there was no stand-alone writing class and that writing was mostly seen as preparation for a high-stakes exam: In describing this situation, she said:

> We didn't write that much. We did only a couple of essays. The longest was, like, 500 words [on a topic like] "Do you think microwaves are good?" They already give you, like, a question and you just have to—they were, like, making sure that you knew how to like the structure a little bit—how to do it.

All three participants from these specialized educational settings, however, described a significant writing project—like a thesis—as a requirement for completion of their program, despite having taken no classes expressly dedicated to writing instruction.

Participants who came from more traditional educational contexts in their home country also noted that they had not taken a specific course for writing prior to matriculating at the U.S. university, although they did have to write in certain content courses. For participants who came from Chinese high schools, writing assignments usually took the form of literary response, taking a stance on a social issue, or writing about a personal experience, as described by Lora:

> Writing, um, like we took Chinese and it's composed reading and writing and some poems and poems analyze . . . topics, um, they are all different but most of them is about Chinese virtue . . . and what should we do to improve our virtue and some are writing about the feelings after you read something. And something to discuss the social problems and writing about your own experience . . . English class . . . is composed by listening, reading, and writing but writing just small part of the poems, like, in an English test . . . so China is focused more on reading and the grammar so the writing side is really short.

For participants who were required to take English as a subject in school, writing was treated as one skill among many—one aspect of a larger academic endeavor—and assignments tended to be short and simple. Amy gave a vivid description of writing in the context of an English language course in a Chinese high school:

> There's no specific writing classes but we have English classes and we focus more mainly on grammar stuff. . . . Writing, yeah, it was so—the writing skills I had at that time, I think it was just American elementary school or middle school level, and we have some, like, essays to write although really, really small essay. Just like tell a story or something. We also have typical type of writing assignments—you have, like, four little pictures, the teacher draws, like, Betty today—Betty goes to the mountain and with her friends and then she saw a whole lot of garbage there and all of her friends are shocked. How could that happen? And then Betty gather her friends and say, "Oh, let's do something" and then they all gonna, like, pick the garbage and then the mountain is clean. Yeah, and all the friends are cheering and they're having a picnic.

The comments of these Chinese participants emphasize both the conventions and epistemologies that underlie writing in their home educational system but also the simplistic exposure they had had to writing in English prior to matriculating at the U.S. university.

In exam-driven educational systems, which were typical for participants in the research pool, mastery of writing was seen as a method of scoring well on high-stakes tests: Luca noted that in her school "the classes prepared you for the exams—that's like basically our whole years from junior to senior were preparing for them. It's not like here in the American system where you just take them . . . it really takes all the year preparation—everything that you work through the year can be in that test."

Several other students also mentioned that "short essays" were practiced in preparation for the English exam. Thus, though writing was clearly a part of all participants' experiences, the phenomenon of a stand-alone course dedicated to writing or composition was unfamiliar to them.

Course Selection: The Theme Matters

Despite the fact that none of the participants had any previous experience with the phenomenon of a class specifically for "writing," they demonstrated a high level of awareness about the weight of the first-year writing requirement at the university. As discussed previously, this particular course is required for undergraduate students at the university, one that most students cannot place or test out of. Even L2 writers who have taken a specialized EAP writing course are required to pass this four-credit mainstream first-year writing course with a grade of C– or higher. The awareness of the weight of the requirement was captured in participant comments about its perceived level of difficulty: "There are a lot of people told me that this class very hard" (Crystal); "My friend . . . asked me which class would you drop if you could and get a full credit out of it? I said FYW definitely . . . I just feel like FYW is really hard. Why would school give a 4.0 credit course when all other courses are 3.0? Which means [it is] going to [be] a really hard time" (Han Gil).

Several participants also commented that they had been apprised in advance of the importance of selecting a course theme that is personally meaningful: "One of my friends . . . took his FYW and he told me that 'Don't pick a course that you didn't interest otherwise you will end with a C because he just ended in a C when he back in freshman year. And then you have to find a topic that interesting yourself first" (Ai); "One of my friends told me that if you really like one topic, don't think if it's hard or easy and, yeah, don't look at ratemyprofessor.com. If you really like something, you just go for it. And I also think that's right because if you find topic not really interest[ing], you don't have the motivation to do research" (Amy). Interestingly, these comments also highlight how prevalent the sharing of information among peers is at the university.

In line with these perceptions, interviews revealed that participants overwhelmingly made thoughtful and strategic decisions about which section to register for. In their own way, all participants gathered intelligence about the course theme, the professor, and the course expectations. Crystal described the process of determining the best-fit course for her:

> Before I choose this class, some classmates of mine . . . has told me that there are several FYW class have less homework and maybe an easier grader, but I think "Oh, I still think I need to improve my writing." I am not confident in my writing so I think maybe I should find some professor who is helpful, so I just go through "rate my professor," which has all the professors here. I use a whole night to choose a FYW class and then I write down about 10 of them who have higher [rating], maybe higher than 4.4 or 4.1 because all the FYW class—a lot of professor get really high score and then I think, "Oh, they are the theme" [and] I think I need to find the theme of the class and then I go for the university writing program [website] and find all the theme about the professor I have chose and then I delete some of them, like, I just can't accept that theme.

A telling description of the selection process also came from Kristen, who said:

> To be honest, I want to find a class that's kind of easy and not a lot of writing. I know it's a writing class (laughter) but . . . someone in sophomore, like, he took that course [that she ended up registering for] last year and last semester actually and he said the teacher is great and the class is kind of interesting and not require a lot of writing . . . I did some research about my professor and also I asked the students who already took FYW.

Han Gil was perhaps the most strategic in relying on intelligence from his network of Korean peers: He tried to register for the class that Korean students had told him was easiest, but all sections of that course were—unsurprisingly—full by the time he tried to register, so he ended up registering for another course that was represented as manageable by his peers. In Michelle's case, where such a network of peers did not exist, she discussed the course theme options on the website with her sister before selecting which course to register for.

Regardless of the extent of research that went into making the decision, participants emphasized how important it was to choose a course topic that was of interest or relevant to them. They frequently commented that the course theme they chose was linked to their personal interests, experiences, or field of study: "I like photography—I took photography two years in high school. I like analyzing different pictures and get a hint of it and also probably I like marketing and probably in the future if I take marketing and I know some basic idea of how to have a powerful images" (Ai); "I think images sound interesting and I think it's maybe useful for our academic writing because like if I like marketing, and advertising is full of images and like charts because we always write about charts, we need to analyze them— I think maybe it's useful" (Crystal); "I just feel like the topic was kind of like unique and sounds like interesting but not I don't really familiar about the topic" (Kristen); "It's architecture and ecology. Because my intended major is architecture and I have already took one semester of the modern architecture design, so I think it will be easier and for me and more useful for me to take this class" (Lora). In one case, this interest was deep and abiding enough for the individual to take on a course that she knew was going to be extremely challenging (Amy, who registered for a course about the Holocaust). She read the descriptions for all of the classes and concluded that this particular class was the only one she "really, really wanted to pursue." She explained:

I am really interested in like historical things and, um, I don't know, I just feel like I have a bond with, like, just the theme of the Holocaust and I also particularly like Jewish people. I don't know why. I just find them really friendly and easy to talk to so, um, and also because the Holocaust was related to Jewish people so I want to choose that topic and also I think this topic was really deep . . . also, um, so after learning this class, I was hoping I could learn more about the Holocaust, learn more about how the Germans did to the Jewish people and learn important life lessons from it. And also I saw other topics like on video games or like horror films or, like, writing without text—it's just not my type. I just don't find any, like—I am just not really interested in that so I just wanted to pursue the Holocaust thing.

Amy engaged in a clear rejection of all other thematic options for the FYW course because she was drawn to the depth and power of a Holocaust-related theme. Her assertion of the personal meaningfulness of this theme also implies that she felt she was different from her peers who may have opted for more "popular," or even easier, topics.

Having determined the best-fit section for themselves in advance, most participants in the study were able to register for their first or second choices for course theme. For Luca and John, however, circumstances beyond their control limited their options. Luca received inaccurate advising advice and was stuck registering for the only course available that fit her schedule, a topic that implied the task of "rewriting" a classic novel: "It was not my favorite choice, but then now that I get to know more the professor, I kind of like it." Due to a registrar error, John ended up in a class about social media rather than the *Mad Men*-themed course he had intended to take:

At first I thought I was taking the *Mad Men* class but then they told me it was changed, that there was a confusion at the registrars so that after now we're gonna to take this about social media. So I was, like, "Oh well, that topic is better" because I had a friend that had the same mistake and he is now stuck in a feminism class so I was like, "Yeah, it could have been worse," so I don't care and I started into the class and I absolutely love it so I was like, "I'm staying here."

Because the course theme was supposed to be so tightly intertwined with the course experience, I asked participants to articulate their understanding of the course topic at the beginning of the semester (see Table 5.1). Though almost every participant was able to summarize his or her understanding of

Table 5.1: Beginning of the Semester: Understanding of the Course Theme and Three Words to Describe the Lived Experience So Far

Pseudonym	Understanding of Course Theme	Words to Describe the Lived Experience		
Han Gil	"how the song influences current issue"	Afraid	Challenge	Excited
Crystal	"images have a different meaning if it has different words under and if it has another picture around them"	Hard	Useful	Busy
Ai	"how images sometimes more powerful than verbal language so they will shape you into a better reader—picture reader"	Happy to get topic	Talkative class	OK ("Don't know what's going on next")
John	"to analyze and write and, like, see how the people sell through social media and how the people use social media to sell, to advertise, and all this stuff to the people"	Shy	Interesting	Being the outsider
Amy	"doing research . . . into the history of what the people in the past have done and what Germans have done to the Jewish race . . . how we can prevent that things happening again in the future"	Attention-grabbing	Delighted	Enlightening

Pseudonym	Understanding of Course Theme	Words to Describe the Lived Experience		
Lora	"architecture is sort of in the environment of it so it must have some connections to ecology and you have to use environmental protection and materials build that buildings and I think it's a thing to do with ecology too so that's the connection"	Hard work	A little confused	Feel I will learn something
Michelle	"It's reading without words; like, we will have book without any words and we will consider what's going on, what is the next and, like, we have to write."	Challenging	Trying/ effort	Analyzing
Kristen	"more about the anthropology and where study, like, the culture in the sport and dance and about the video game"	Surprising	Different/ Interesting	Sharing
Yoono	"It is mostly about food . . . stories of people's habits and cooking styles."	Intense	Slow (time goes slowly during class)	Challenging
Luca	"I thought it's going to be, like, talking about the book all the semester and, like, rewriting it which I didn't know—if it's already written, why would I like to change it?"	Surprising	Curious	Girly

the course topic, these descriptions were often accompanied by some uncertainty: "Kind of confused. I have even considered changing class" (Han Gil); "I thought the course would be a lot of talking about a lot of—yeah it would be about culture and politics and food as well but what I learned is that most of the class is actually about food . . . I'm still trying to figure it out" (Yoono); "I thought it's going to be like talking about the book [*Jane Eyre*] all the semester and like rewriting it which I didn't know—if it's already written, why would I like to change it? I mean yet, I don't know how that's going to work out. I don't know how we're going to rewrite yet because so far, we talked about like different types of rewriting, about criticism or parodies, stuff like that, but I'm not sure how that fits with *Jane Eyre*" (Luca); "I am still crazy about the course, what will happen next and now I am just struggling to understand images like etchings and something like that. Now I can't understand everything from the paintings but maybe a couple of weeks after, I will understand this" (Michelle).

Participants were also asked to choose three words that described their experience in the FYW class so far. As Table 5.1 indicates, some of the words and phrases chosen clearly illustrate anxiety, yet we can also see an openness and a curiosity; perhaps Han Gil's response perfectly captures the mix of emotions students felt in entering this new environment: "afraid and excited." Some responses highlight a sense of curiosity and openness to engagement: "surprising," "enlightening," "interesting," "sharing," "talkative." A number of the words also reflect participants' awareness that this course is a particularly rigorous requirement: "intense," "challenging," "hard, hard work," "effort," "busy." Crystal said: "Even Americans say this class is hard"; Han Gil noted that it's the one class in his schedule that he has anxiety about: "Cause if you look at my schedule math, I think I can do it. Macro[economics], I am confident [in] and Business Administration is just talking, which is really easy . . . I was going to major in Bio and Chem, so it is totally fine. But FYW is always just a challenge for me." Even Yoono, who had a high level of confidence in his ability to manage the course, mentioned not wanting to have to "write big papers under pressure from other courses." In other words, relative to the other courses the participants were taking, this writing class was perceived as particularly rigorous and challenging, and participants' impressions at the beginning of the semester capture the combination of hopefulness and interest with uncertainty and confusion.

Self-Perception within a Socio-Academic Space

The final theme from participants' entry point into the class derived from their situatedness in this particular socio-academic environment. To better understand participants' self-perception *within* this space, it is important to have a sense of how they described the classroom environment. Overwhelmingly, participants noted the small class size and the high level of discussion and interaction; many described sitting in a "U" shape or semicircle in the classroom. Ai's comment captures a number of shared elements in participants' description of the classroom environment:

> I actually feel I sort of really comfortable in my class. We have 15 students and we talk and the professor . . . at the beginning he said this is not a lecture-based course—it's more a student discussion course so you want to share your opinions since way of seeing people have different idea of it and if you can speak up and people can share different story, that can enhance your view of different point of view . . . open atmosphere . . . U-shape and teacher in the middle . . . mostly American students [talking].

Others added that the atmosphere was informal and relaxed, and that all students were expected to participate in activities and discussions. According to John, this size and nature of the class made him feel closer to his professor and classmates: "You kind of like get to know everyone in the class . . . 'Cause there's a lot of interaction in the small classes cause they make you talk to each other, like, there's discussion between things so you kind of getting related and it's, like, oh, this guy is like me, I should talk to him," which was a sentiment that was echoed in other participant comments at the beginning of the semester. Kristen noted that "everyone gets a chance to talk and discuss, and so it's pretty good."

In some cases, however, the discussion appeared to be more dominated by the professor; for example, Amy described her professor as a "storyteller" and that there is "not much discussion but more like student interacting with the professor and because we were all so impressed about the stories and it's really heavy, so the class is not, like, that active, [with a] student saying his views or her point of views." One participant, on the other hand, observed that her professor encouraged a little too much participation on the part of students: When the professor asked a question, she said, "A lot of people hand up but something I just can't understand why students repeat someone other's opinion in another way." She viewed this type of thing as class time being wasted. So although there was some discrepancy in the balance of participation in class discussions, it was evident that there was a great deal of commonality in participants' rendering of the classroom atmosphere.

Within this socio-academic framework, participants were asked in interviews to reflect on their "place" within this environment. The overwhelming theme that emerged here was that, for these participants, their senses of self in this setting was relational, shaped by their perception of their abilities or understandings relative to their peers in the class. In some cases, examples of this related to content knowledge about the course theme. For example, Amy, who was taking a class about the Holocaust, said she remained quiet in class: "Because I all I do is just, like, absorbing knowledge because I don't know anything about this topic. And if the topic is about, like, Nanking Holocaust, I know many things about that but Jewish things, hmm, I still need to do many research about it." Crystal perceived that the American students who spoke in class must know more about the topic than she does: "They [American students] just say about their opinions so it's fine but American students just, like, they have a lot to talk and some of them I think maybe they are really good at art because they can think of a lot of art—like, they can say, 'Oh Mona Lisa uses this kind of things' and I think, 'Oh are you an art major?'" Kristen attributed her quietness in the classroom to anxiety about saying the wrong thing: "I feel like some

American students . . . are more like to answer the questions . . . sometimes I feel I don't understand the topic a lot since I don't play the same [games] and am, um, kind of afraid I say something wrong." Michelle articulated a similar reticence until she understood the topic better: "Maybe sometime later I will participate class actively every time because, like, now I am concentrating about my topics and so I am not sure about my opinion is true or false." This anxiety of not being able to speak about the topic extended to concerns about vocabulary:

> Sometimes I can't understand him [the professor], like some specific professional words in that class and I was a little—I didn't ask because other students are Americans and they may understand and it may be a stupid question to ask that in more words because my vocabulary was not as much good as them so , . . . like, not only architecture words, like, some normal words, like, Americans think normal but to me it's, I don't know what that means. Once my professor asks my classmates, do you guys know "Blah, blah, blah" and they are, like, yes, yeah, yeah, yeah. And I was, like, "What is that?" (Lora)

Lora did note, however, an incident that shifted her self-perception. She was having a small-group discussion in which she shared some architectural knowledge that her group mates did not have and was able to help the group analyze an architectural structure in the way the professor expected. She described feeling a "kind of relief because, like, they are not so good as I thought it would be and I feel like I can keep up with the class with them. At least we are, like, the same." In other words, her self-perception shifted once she realized that she had knowledge to share with her peers and that they did not have the level of expertise she had assumed, which highlights the situational and relational nature of such perceptions.

In terms of relational self-perception, others attributed silence in the classroom to cultural characteristics, such as Michelle, who commented that "American students participate very actively and in my opinion [the] Asian students [are] really quiet class," and Han Gil, who said, "I can clearly tell Asians talk less than native speakers 'cause when he [the professor] asks questions, it is always native answering the questions rather than the Asians. Even though he told us you have to talk in class otherwise you will not receive your participation point, we'll still not talk." Participants also frequently implied that "native" (L1) speakers were somehow more qualified to speak out during class because their level of English was so much better: Ai described himself as "more of a listener than a speaker in this class. When Americans speak . . . they can speak better language than you." For Lora, this manifested itself as a fear of not being understood when she spoke in class: "I mean, I can understand what they are talking about but, like, when I interact with them, I still a little weak and when I say something that they can't quite understand, they say, 'What, what did you say?' I was less confident." And for others, such as Crystal, they felt like they lacked the listening comprehension skills to engage fully with class discussions, especially because some American students speak so quickly.

Similarly, because L1 speakers jumped into discussions so freely, some participants felt they had lost their opportunity to contribute. Ai, for example, commented that "probably some American students, they know this topic before, so they actually spoke a lot and sometimes they got my idea first already and I don't think I should raise my hand again anymore because I don't want to repeat that idea again"; Crystal said, "Every time that I finally find out how to say my opinion in English, someone has said something similar with mine so I just give up to say that because someone has said that . . . you feel so confident to speak but just there like Americans, they talk so fast. Before you have prepared, they have said a lot."

Luca and Han Gil both extended this comparative sense of anxiety to their perceptions of expectations for writing. Luca had been raised in a multilingual environment and was quite confident in her spoken English, and Han Gil had been attending an English-medium school since the age of 12. Both emphasized in their interview that, while other international students were intimidated by speaking up in a classroom of American peers, they themselves believed mistakes were a natural part of the process and had much less hesitation about speaking out. When it came to writing, however, both told a different story. According to Luca, "I feel that I am the minority there when it comes to being international, like, I feel like I am less experienced than the other girls so I feel that sometimes that can be kind of, like, scary to be compared with their types of writing. I mean girls that are there, they kind of know what they are doing. They have taken English classes." One described the sense of intimidation when, on the first day of class, the instructor told the class that previous student assignments had been posted on the class website (Blackboard) as models:

> He gave us all the past essay which is posted in Blackboard, so he made us read them. And I read all of them. I read all of them. He said only, like, first few to read but I read all of them just to see how good the people are and I know I cannot write like that. It is such a high level for me . . . the essay written, it has all the names on it, too. But none of them are Asian so I feel like, yeah (laughter). It is even more pressure.

For this student, what was probably designed to be a helpful resource—access to model papers written by former students—became a major stressor from the beginning of the semester.

Other participant comments revealed how differently they would have behaved or perceived themselves in a classroom setting in their home community. Michelle stated that she tended not to speak up during her writing class in the United States, but, "If I were in Mongolia, I will participate very actively because I am using my first language, but in my second language, sometimes I feel shy or how will they react to my English or something like that." John recalled being considered a strong speaker and writer of English in Ecuador, but coming into FYW course, his confidence was undermined:

Especially when I'm trying to participate in class, I kind
of feel like I have an accent and everything so when I
talk, the people don't—and if I make a mistake, cause
I usually, like, little bit stutter in English, when I make
a mistake, the people, like, see it. . . . I don't know how
to say—I feel down, like, "Oh, I shouldn't participate."
I should just let this guy talk and, they know how to
talk. I just pay attention, stuff like that, so it is kind of,
like, that part—the class participation kind of under-
mines me a little bit. I don't like to participate because
of that—I don't know. . . . Usually in Ecuador, you talk
in Spanish or in English there and it's, like, "Oh, yeah,
you're good, you're fine." Unless you say a really stupid
thing, it's going to be fine whatever you say. Here, even
if you say a really nice thing, like, a really intelligent or
a really constructive thing, you comment, they will say,
like, "Oh yeah, this guy speaks, like, real low." Did you
see the mistake he made? He didn't use the past tense
or something like that . . . it gets even worse when the
teacher doesn't get it or you don't express, like, really
good your idea, so I got really nervous in that sense. I
was just, like, "Oh, never mind, never mind" . . . Yeah,
next time I should just skip it.

John's comments here are a good example of his journey: In his
home community he was confident speaking in both Spanish
and English and did not feel self-conscious interacting with
his peers. In the U.S. classroom setting, however, he became so
aware of his "accent" and his grammar errors that he was often
reduced to silence.

Of the participants, Yoono was the only one who did not
compare himself unfavorably to his "American" peers in the
classroom: "I feel I fit in. Uh, I feel based on my level of English that I am capable of doing well in the class. I feel I am
within the same range of level with the kids who are already
there and yeah, I feel comfortable in the class." Even though his

self-assessment was positive relative to his peers, it is still clear that his experience aligns with the broader theme of participants' self-view being shaped by their perception of how they compare with peers in that particular setting.

In several cases, the presence of a friend from the same cultural background—or even just another international student—gave comfort and confidence to participants. Kristen and John both selected their FYW class with a close friend from their home country; as John said: "I think it's always nice to know someone in the class. It kind of gives you confidence." Amy noted that having a Jewish friend in the Holocaust class with her gave her a sense of security, and when Lora arrived at the first day of class, she was relieved to see three other Chinese international students there: "It's kind of like make me feel relief because I'm not the only international student who can't speak so fluently and I'm kind of speak better (laughter). It's kind of given me some confidence." For Luca, the fact that her class about *Jane Eyre* was predominantly composed of females made her feel "more comfortable" and "able to make friends," and in particular the presence of another international student who had gone to high school in Maryland made her feel she had an ally.

When students were asked to look ahead to the rest of the semester, similar patterns of response emerged. They described their expectations in terms of what they "hoped" to learn: for example, "to be more comfortable, participate more actively" (Michelle); "to be a better writer" (Luca); "to study more about a different field" (Kristen); "really focusing for an A . . . learn a lot about myself, about how the people interact in the social media network" (John); "maybe make my writing just more like American style, not too much Chinglish" (Crystal). However, when they expressed their concerns, an anxiety about managing what they perceived as the writing expectations for the class emerged. Michelle said: "I am worrying about first essay, what would it be, like, what will be the topic because, like, writing in second language is very challenging and difficult so all the time

I am worrying about writings," Luca emphasized: "Writing is always my concern," and Han Gil mentioned:

> I always think, like, my essay is really horrible . . . I mean I try my best obviously. I try multiple of times. It just—first I think in Korean, then in English, right? And the translation is really difficult. And some things we express in Korean, I cannot express in English, so yeah. Sometimes it is really unclear, my essays. 'Cause it makes sense to me, but it doesn't make sense to others.

Even Yoono, who entered the class with a high level of confidence in his own abilities, commented that he wanted to be able to concentrate on his writing assignments for this class without being weighed down by work from his other classes. It would appear that although the course theme was a key element in course selection and early class discussions, the specter of writing was hovering over participants as they finished the first two weeks of the class.

6

Negotiating the FYW Experience: Interactions

This chapter targets participants' experiences at the mid-point of the semester in which they were enrolled in the first-year writing class. I saw this part of the semester as a point of saturation: Participants had been part of the class for seven to eight weeks and were continuing to make sense of the course and their place within the classroom, but had largely developed an understanding of the class and its expectations. Based on these understandings, it was clear that participants were *negotiating* this socio-academic experience, both in terms of their engagement with the course theme and class activities and in terms of their interactions in the classroom setting.

The themes developed as a result of these interviews show an evolving understanding but at the same time are coherent to both the data from the first round of interviews and to what I infer to be each participant's *process* of engaging with the experience. Under the umbrella of the overarching theme of negotiating the experience through interactions, this chapter outlines the second-interview themes of (1) interaction with the course theme; (2) being "on the ball"; and (3) highs and lows.

Level of Interaction with the Course Theme

It was clear from the first interview that the course theme was a key factor in participants' course selection decision and that it

Figure 6.1: Negotiating the Socio-Academic Space

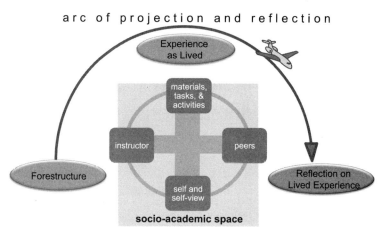

shaped their early impressions of the class and their place within it. Participant responses during the second interview reinforced the significance of the course theme on the experience. Day-to-day activities clearly revolved around that topic, with students reporting that they prepared for class through assigned readings or short informal writings about the course theme. As an example, Lora described a typical class in this way:

> We discuss the material the professor gives us before that day, like, last class he give us and the materials he asked us to read and connect that to the topic that we are discussing in this module and analyze some similar thoughts of authors online. He just opens some pages online and asks us to read and analyze how they're similar or the difference between this passages and the materials he give us . . . sometimes he asks us to write, like, 100 words, short paragraph.

Most classroom activities seemed to be centered on the course's thematic content, and descriptions of the course theme indicate a growing sophistication in participants' understanding. Compared to the beginning of the semester, participants were far better able to articulate the course's thematic focus, as demonstrated in these three quotes:

Food, culture, and power theme: You know I [thought] it's mainly about food but one thing I realized was that it's not really food in relation to one thing; it's been food in relation to many different things and that's seen through our papers. Basically, our papers involve doing ethnographic style research where basically you have to interview participants and your research was based off—your paper was based on comparing and contrasting and making conclusions based on what your participants told you. And all of our papers actually had to do with food but each one's paper had to do with a different element of food. Ours, for example, had to do with the effect travel could have on one's cooking habits and styles. (Yoono)

Interpreting images theme: Now I have better understanding of image because when I registered this class, I have no idea about it, just image as text and then, like, now I know that we can read the image and I can do it, which I want because some other courses, like in science, there is wrong or right so I say the image is just sharing your thoughts and connecting to some theory or something like that, yeah. . . . Every assignment, the first assignment that professor gave us the lens, the book. You have graphic novel and you have to use another book as a lens. To read this book, you have read this book, like, the understanding comics or something particular book and we will first look at our graphic novel. Then read the understanding comics . . . then how it's applied to this graphic novel, and but in the second time, we have to choose own lens, it's more broad, like, psychology and sociology. And so if I choose one picture and if I want to write the aspect of psychology, I have to find the psychology books which is very relevant to the image. (Michelle)

Social media theme: It's basically like an overview of how people, any company, people, like famous artist, whatever personality, how they brand themselves, how they sell, how they promote and connect with the fans through social media, how they use this new tool to get everyone involved. By everyone, I mean the fans. It's a new way to socialize. For example, years ago, when a famous artist all this stuff went to make an announcement, they would go to a press release, everything on TV. They now are Twitter or post something on Facebook. This is kind of, like, a new science for marketing all this stuff—PR and everything, so it basically involves every industry there is, so it's kind of, like, you learn kind of a science. It's a completely new type of subject, everything that basically involves all our random marketing and all this stuff, advertising, branding. (John)

These examples demonstrate that participants were developing not just a descriptive understanding of the course theme but also a new way of *looking at* the topic both conceptually and practically. This deeper understanding of the course theme was often enhanced by interactions with others; for example Ai, who was taking a class about interpreting images, said, "Everybody picks different painting . . . so it's actually really helpful that when we look at one painting together, I hear different thoughts from others [that] actually can change my thinking. And when I look at my own piece, I'm trying to [consider] 'Oh, how did that guy think that way?' so I think a different way on my piece of painting, so yeah, basically a lot of discussion." Han Gil, whose FYW course had a music theme, noted, "Everyone give different opinion and then I can think 'Oh, that person thinks like that, but I think like this' so I can compare. So it's like open discussion, right. So I like that part of the class."

Though it was clear that their grasp of the course theme was increasing, what participants perceived as the accessibility of the topic, or of its subtopics, also affected the experience. For instance, Crystal spoke with greater fluency about the course theme and seemed to have increased her ability to analyze images better but noted that, even with those skills, she often lacked the cultural knowledge to understand the context for the images they worked with in class:

> That one is really hard because without the word, it's just hard to figure out what does it mean. It's, like, well sometimes you read the context, it really tell you something behind the picture, behind the painting. . . . The two examples her gave us, like, she give us this one of an African American, another one is for Declaration of Freedom? [Declaration of Independence] That's very deep meaning, but without knowing, like, some American history and other things, it's harder.

Han Gil mentioned not knowing as much about American pop culture as his classmates did:

> I feel like I don't know much about America, I'm not from U.S. school or something, I studied in India so I don't know many artists. Like, if I ask any of my classmates who Beyonce or, like, who's Jay Z or whatever, they'll tell us, like, from their head . . . but I cannot. I know they are artists, but I don't know who they are, I don't know who they're married to, I don't know what they did. I'm not used to that stuff you know, but if I were told to write about Korean rapper, Korean artist, I can definitely write better cause I know more about it.

Similarly, Kristen, who was taking a course on gesture and sport, said: "Sometimes I feel like, 'Oh, that's interesting and I don't know that before,' but for a negative part is that I really don't know a lot of things about sports but I have to write about them." These quotes highlight a perceived lack of understanding due to gaps in cultural knowledge.

Lora described how her interest in the course theme shifted when she realized that the focus was less on architecture and more on urban planning: "First day, I thought it was going to be like my last class, like, find some typical building and talk about how they related to the nature because in my class last semester, talk about the beauty which is, like, organic building, organic architecture but it comes to the urban planning now." Luca talked about how, despite not really liking the book *Jane Eyre*, she had to find a way to focus her writing topics on aspects of the book she could connect with:

> I would try to do the best with what I'm given and how they say, like, if we try to pull what we like of the book in order to write something. For example, I based it on a new version of *Jane Eyre*, which I like better so that's, like, try to find what I do like about the paper and write it about the subject. It has to be like that because if not then I wouldn't reflect a good grade. I mean you have to put the effort so for that you have to try to find something that you like or else it would be awful.

This connection worked in the opposite direction as well: Both John and Amy, who selected their own research topics early in the semester, described themselves as highly engaged in their own topics of study and drawn into the broader course theme based on students' sharing information and ideas about their individual topics.

An interesting finding related to engagement with the theme was the extent to which participants described the classroom experience in the first half of the semester as being dominated by reading and discussion and less by writing. In fact, the high expectations for reading played an important role in their experience in the FYW class. In describing their experiences reading for class, participants clearly distinguished "easy" reading (model student essays, blogs and other websites, personal narratives, or popular press) from "challenging" reading (theoretical or other scholarly texts), as illustrated in these quotes: "Sometimes we have some student essays, so we read it. I think proofreading a student's essay is easier than other kind of academic or scholarly reading because it may be we are from the same generation and they use some easy words instead of some big word or difficult word and also the tone of the writing is—from the reading—it's actually kind of more casual" (Ai); "Some of them [short current articles about social media] are really good and you can understand what they, like the point the author in that article must make and everything a . . . sometimes there are, like, really bad or, like, kind of, like, use complex words and all this stuff. Like, it's kind of, like, too technical, so it's kind of, like, hmmm 'I don't get it, like what is she trying to do, like trying to say here?'" (John); "That was awful because they were very long readings and many of them, because they were written by scholars, they used like very fancy vocabulary so I had— it was like very frustrating for me sometimes to understand the point because I didn't understand the vocabulary and it wasn't me, the only one. Even for, like, native English speakers, it was hard to follow the point. So that was not easy" (Luca). Several participants also noted how long it took them to do the reading, especially of the more academic texts, and the anxiety this provoked: "Sometimes I can't finish the reading I don't even talk about anything [in class] and I'm afraid that my professor find out that I didn't read it" (Lora).

Though the influence of reading on the course experience was evident, writing was still mentioned; by the midpoint in the semester, most students had completed a series of informal writing tasks, such as blogs, discussion board posts, or brief quick-writes on a reading, and one or two individual or group essays. Luca, like others, had anxiety about the "big" project that takes place during the second half of the semester: "I'm already scared of what is going to be the other paper. I have no idea"; Kristen described her previous assignments as being group essays and was uncertain about what the "big" individual research paper would entail; Michelle perceived the last paper as the "most difficult. I think it's the research paper like the 12–15 pages." Even those who were more comfortable with their topics, such as John, who was writing about social media as it related to his favorite soccer team, saw this major project as intimidating:

We are starting Monday the 17-page long essays, so I don't know yet how hard it's going to be, but our project is gonna be about my soccer team, so, like, I have to make a critique and everything, how they should improve all this stuff so I am kind of confident that the topic is not going to be hard, but it's still 17 pages long and it's in English so it's not going to be that easy either. . . . I know it going to be hard but I think I'm growing confident that the last essay, that's 40% of the grade, that's what makes it kind of scary . . . that's almost 50% of the final grade so if I mess it up, like, the whole grade is going to go down, but I think I'm going to do pretty good.

However, despite the concern about what was ahead, there seemed to be a growing sense of manageability, as captured in this statement by Ai:

Every time I finish up I say I will be excited, like, I just finished my first essay even though I don't know my score of the essay, I still, "Oh, I finished up one essay, two more to go." And then you know I think it's kind of mild storm, oh, you finish one, yeah and then to come out, you're really struggling and then when you finish, oh, second and I say one more and then you graduate. . . . my international student and all my friends in the FYW class and they are very trying to also find their self in because, you know, writing is definitely, writing in your second language is definitely difficult for us. Also when actually when I didn't take the course and I heard people talking about it, oh, 15 pages, 17 pages and I thought no way and I cannot write it—no it's not for me, I cannot write 15 or 20 pages like that, but after we kind of finished different text and different assignments, I kind of feel you actually can see yourself doing that way even though you are not 100%; you can do it but when you finish something, "Oh, 5 pages, I did it," and then maybe next time 8 pages, and maybe in the future 15 pages.

This captures not only the negotiation of academic tasks but also participants' growing confidence in being able to manage them; though Ai still displays some uncertainty at the end ("even though you are not 100%" and "maybe in the future"), he has clearly exceeded his initial expectations of what he was capable of.

Being "On the Ball"

The second theme under negotiating interactions in the FYW classroom is related to participation in a dynamic classroom environment. As discussed, participants felt pressure to keep up with readings and to come to class prepared, and this expectation to be "on the ball" and active contributors clearly influenced participants' experiences. At the midpoint in the semester, the description of the classroom environment and its day-to-day tasks and activities was fairly consistent with participants' impression of the class at the beginning of the semester. Each participant painted a picture of a classroom where ideas were constantly moving and conveyed a certain amount of pressure to participate; Yoono described it as a class where "everybody is focused," and Ai mentioned the professor's expectation that everyone "speak up." For Crystal, this expectation had a "forced" dimension: "It's a kind of way that force you to participate in the class, but now it's just like [I] cannot get used to it, to say something because you always know that 'Oh, I have to say something.'" Even in small group discussions, there was pressure to participate:

> Actually I'm the one that kind of listens more because first, um, I don't, I would say maybe because of my language problem, well I—hmm, it's just there is not much chance for me to say it say something because, like, my group mates are all, like, very talkative so they talk and—I did provide many ideas to them and they'll coordinate and say it in class. . . . Sometimes if I didn't contribute much to the group, I will feel a little bit uncomfortable. But if I did contribute to the group, then I'm fine with it . . . because

I feel like everyone should say something and should contribute. (Amy)

In many ways the discussion-oriented approach seemed to make participants feel they were part of the class, but no one referred to him- or herself as a dominant member of the class; instead they considered themselves more like occasional contributors. Those with higher levels of fluency in English did not mention any challenges following the discussions but were still thoughtful and somewhat guarded in what they said; for example, Yoono said that he tried to speak every class and that "when I have an idea that makes sense, I will say it; otherwise I don't have a need to speak," and John noted that, though he does participate two to three times per class, "I learn more from them [classmates] than they do from me." Luca noted a qualified confidence about joining in class discussions: "Of course . . . when you're an international student, when you talk you feel very conscious about your sayings, especially in class. When there are different people around, sometimes I feel conscious about—like, 'Am I saying it right, is it okay?' but . . . now that I know the professor, I feel more comfortable talking." Students who perceived themselves as having lower levels of proficiency, such as Crystal, described the experience of keeping up with class discussions as overwhelming because her American classmates spoke so fast:

You have to keep your mind there, have a high focus, easy to get lost, uncomfortable if you say something someone else said . . . the professor is always easier to understand than the student because the students, they use some kind of word and they sometimes speak fast. I think the professor [has] the intent to make it not so fast because I just find all the professors, they have a common speed, like, not too fast so it's easy to understand. But some students, they get so excited (laughter) and they just speak so fast.

In keeping up with the pace of the class, a number of participants faced the same struggles they described at the beginning of the semester, notably that by the time they got their thoughts together to speak in English, another student had already said what they wanted to say: "Sometimes even I want to contribute something to class and I can't express it in English, like, I can't find a proper word to say it" (Lora); "Sometimes it's like I have an idea but the American students answer quickly and then say it so I don't need to repeat it. Yeah but sometimes I tell my opinions" (Michelle). This perception of limitation provoked a number of responses on the part of participants. Ai said he tried to raise his hand to speak on occasion but that when he spoke it was very brief and simple compared to what his American classmates would say; thus he concluded: "I am going to learn instead of sharing. I kind of want to absorb the knowledge from others while they are talking." He also emphasized that he was comfortable speaking out on topics that were casual or personal but that on scholarly or academic topics, he was much less likely to speak.

Kristen described a strategic response to what she considered the dilemma of participation: "I remember last time I tell you I don't really want to talk for this class since a lot of people, like, they're more active than I am and they more likely to talk so, but after I find out everyone have to say something what they think interesting and the chapter is not that long so now I try to—I speak early—I try to raise my hand and to explain my idea before other people do so." One participant's strategic response to participating in class derived from a desire to distance himself from fellow students from his home country who frequently spoke in their native language during class. He felt that the professor got "annoyed by them" and that he—by extension— would be painted with the same brush. As a result, he sat next to the professor in class and tried to participate without engaging with his home country peers.

In conclusion, all participants described an active classroom environment and expressed, in various ways, how they responded to this expectation to be "on the ball" in the FYW class. Though there was an occasional mention of a tense interaction, participants overwhelmingly characterized the environment as respectful, as captured in this quote by John: "When we talk, like, in class everybody participates and kind of, like, 'Yeah, I think you are wrong because. . . . ' It's really polite; they have a lot of respect for each other and it's not, like, for example in Ecuador when we debate and discuss something, the class will start yelling stuff and standing up saying, 'No, you're wrong!' Here it's like, 'No, you're wrong because. . . .'" These descriptions of day-to-day class activities clearly reinforce the extent to which classroom *interactions* shaped participants' understanding of this lived experience.

Highs and Lows

During the second interview, participants were asked to narrate examples of what they considered positive and negative experiences in FYW. Positive experiences related by participants directly linked to the "reception" that they felt others gave to their ideas. Crystal gave an example of pointing out an aspect of an image that no one else in the class had noticed, and then being given positive feedback from her professor and having other students build on the comment she had made. John described an idea he mentioned in class being well received by his professor, who later encouraged him to put it in his essay as an example, and several other participants noted feeling encouraged when their professors responded favorably to what they said in class. As Michelle said, "I think that the professor is very kind person, like, when I tell him my opinion or, like, [ask a] favor, he never refuse it or never get down my opinions, like, always encouraging." Amy discussed a time when she stayed after class to speak to her professor and shared with her a story related to something they had discussed in class: "I told my professor about it and she is so moved by it and I also recommend a film to her." These types of positive interactions seemed to carry a great deal of weight for participants.

Participants also described the receptiveness of their classmates to their ideas as a positive element of the class. For example, Yoono felt good about a very successful discussion he led: "First of all, I got a good grade and besides that a lot of good discussions were fed off that presentation . . . people understood and were listening to what I was saying." Ai had a similar feeling of satisfaction when he led a class discussion: "I think today I feel really positive from my presentation today and you know, standing in front of class and talking your second language to the whole class and then when I hear people respond to my questions, I feel really happy because they know what I mean." Before beginning the research, I had assumed that L2 students might be self-conscious sharing their work with others and critiquing the work of their peers. Surprisingly, however, peer review or writing groups frequently came up as a positive experience for participants, with comments about how they felt the experience connected them to their classmates and improved their writing: "At first I felt a little nervous, like, I was curious about what they will tell about my paper and they gave me very precious advice to improve my idea and improve my writing, yeah . . . I think that there were American students and I like their writing style and so I did the advice as can I do so" (Michelle); "Oh, maybe this [the draft he had not felt confident about] is workable" (Han Gil, on getting complimented on his writing by his peers); "more confident about the things I turn in to teacher" (Kristen). Amy and Luca both described feeling amazed at the level of support their peers provided:

> I found that the students there are, they are really responsible. They're really—so I felt a little ashamed about—like, I only finished the peer review rubric, that is the obligated, mandatory thing . . . but my peer, she actually printed out all my paper and that was—I wrote a really long paper, around like 15 pages. She print them all and do, like, detailed notes and cross out things and add things in my paper. (Amy)

> Amazingly, I thought for my second draft, that was like a writing group and some of my classmates read it and

analyzed the citations they were correct or the content and they didn't say it was that bad—I mean they said it was good sort of. I thought my paper was awful but they had better opinion of my paper than I did . . . I did like [peer review] because I mean sometimes you tend to be very harsh on your paper and probably I think that I'm insecure because I'm not, like, American speaker (laughter), English speaker or, like, I don't have the same knowledge when it comes to writing in English so I'm very insecure when it comes to that . . . but then when my friends read it [and said], "No, it's actually interesting; you need to structure it better or do this, correct that," so that was a really good experience that I liked a lot. . . . It also kind of also helped me to see how they wrote and how I could, like, also write myself. It was a good example for me and, yeah, the girls that I got, they are really good writers so I was kind of happy that I had them as an example. (Luca)

Luca, Amy, and several other participants seemed surprised—and even touched—that their classmates were so willing to help them with their drafts.

Lows were similarly linked to how their contributions compared to what they perceived as their peers' abilities, an extension of the previously developed theme about relational self-perception. In other words, even though they had been in the class seven or eight weeks, participants were still negotiating where they "fit" in this socio-academic environment. In some cases, it was a struggle not to be seen as one of the worst in the class. Ai said, "I'm trying to find myself . . . when there was 15 students, you know maybe the first three or four, they are really talkative and in the professor's mind and then I definitely don't want to be at the end. I don't want the 15th or the 14th." Crystal also commented on not wanting to be on the "bottom" and feeling more pressure than she had in the EAP class she had taken the previous semester:

You get more nervous because you know that—because in the EAP class, I know . . . my writing. It's not the best, but it's, like, middle . . . but here, it's, like, "Oh, I should try my best or maybe I'll be the worst" because I just find even Chinese students in that class, they have high school in here or someone take international high school, so I think, "Oh, they are just, like, they know better, they know a lot than me." So it's just, like, you pay much more attention to it.

Lora implied that she learned a lesson about being understood based on her observation of a Chinese classmate who was not shy about speaking out but was rarely understood: "Every time after he talk, like, the professor looks like confused . . . sometimes I don't even know what he's talking about." Ai described a negative feeling he had when he could not contribute in the way he felt he should:

Maybe sometimes for discussion and, like, when I'm reading some heavy—when my professor assigned some reading overnight and when we have a really heavy reading, I personally am a slow reader and I maybe took a long time. Maybe American students only take 20 minutes to finish. I may take up to 45 minutes maybe devote of time, and sometimes I maybe didn't get the inner meaning of the reading or maybe only on the surface so it sometimes will be difficult for me to join the discussion and then talk with them. And I maybe feel frustrated if—I know my professor want everyone to speak up but maybe my professor may understand American students— I actually did talk to my professor but I tried to understand the passage on my own, but if it did happen in that situation, I'm just going to be silent during that discussion, but I don't—you know, when you are really silent in discussion, you feel kind of not in it and sort of the feeling not really good.

Michelle talked about this pressure as it extended to writing: "Because we have to write same as the American students, like, the level is, like, have to be the same so every time when I get assignment, like, say I have to spend more time than Americans because some Americans maybe can do a paper on only one or two nights yeah, but we can't do it." Though Han Gil expressed occasional frustration with his experience in the FYW class, he made an interesting comment about his own responsibility for the position he was in relative to his American peers: "I cannot complain because I'm the one who chose to come abroad and study, you know. And if I want to study or write, I should be as good as the locals here, right, because they're the ones studying, so I try my best to improve, improve, improve."

Participants' concern about how their ideas were responded to also extended to the submission of drafts for writing assignments, with "lows" often characterized by perceptions engendered by feedback they received from their professors. A participant described the experience of getting feedback on the first draft of a rhetorical analysis as:

> Pretty much change everything, like, it's really bad . . . that kind of get me down 'cause I thought it was—I know it was bad, like, kind of disorganized—but I think the ideas were good, but the way that she [the professor] didn't like—well, I don't try to blame the teacher but the fact that my ideas weren't, like—well, this is a good idea, you should try to rephrase it or something like that. Instead, like, no this is really disorganized—she was kind of looking into the way it was organized rather than what I was trying to say, so that kind of get me down.

Based on comments she received on her first draft, Crystal described her essay as "kind of a disaster; professor find a lot of weak points (not so many good points)," leaving her feeling she had lots of work to do and that the standards for writing in the class were extremely high. For Lora, though she had felt her grammar was not that bad when she wrote her draft, she said, "When I saw his [the professor's] feedback, there are really a lot, and he's, like, he can't, like, point every grammar mistake to me because this course is not based on that; but he said that he is going to give, like, four of us, the international students a grammar section or something like that, but he doesn't email us yet." One participant even explained that no matter how hard he tried, he felt could not meet the expectation his professor had for his assignments and that he received feedback that said his writing "made no sense" or was "unclear" but that he was hoping for more concrete guidance on how to improve: "I mean I don't care about the grade, as long as [the professor] give out proper feedback, as long as [the professor] tell me what to do now, I'll fix it."

Other participants also made mention of being confused or unsure about how to approach a writing assignment or having challenges interpreting instructor feedback. Amy discussed her feelings of confusion this way: "I was kind of confused about what I'm going to write and even during the peer review, for the whole peer review, I was really confused about what I am going to write." Luca noted feeling confused and overwhelmed by the level of detail in her assignment prompt, and then when she got the feedback on her draft, she found the professor's comments to be "very long and very detailed," which sometimes made her feel "lost in it . . . the way [the professor] explain it was with very sophisticated vocabulary with words, like, sometimes I really don't know what she's saying." We can see here that, though some of the "lows" participants shared related to their self-perception or ability to keep up with their peers, a number are linked to the actual purpose of the class: the writing assignments and the reception of their written work by others.

7

Reflections on the Lived Experience:
You Get What You Put In

This chapter highlights findings from the third set of interviews, which were timed to coincide with participants' exit from the FYW class. It was during these interviews that they were asked to reflect on the overall experience and what they would be taking away from it. The broad theme that emerged from these reflections was "you get what you put in," which appeared to derive from the cumulative experience of being a part of a class like this and a sense of satisfaction at being able to manage course expectations. The themes of (1) the influence of the socio-academic environment; (2) course theme versus writing; and (3) a sense of accomplishment were revealed and will be discussed in the remainder of this chapter.

The Influence of the Socio-Academic Environment

By the final interview, all participants in some way echoed Michelle's comment that "of course this class was very challenging" and acknowledged the heavy workload, but there was also an overall commonality in their descriptions regarding the ways that the atmosphere and interactions in the classroom shaped their experiences. Through all three interviews, participants painted a picture of a classroom that was highly interactive, where students sat in a circle and were expected to be "on the ball" and share their ideas with others. Yoono characterized the

Figure 7.1: Reflecting on the Socio-Academic Experience

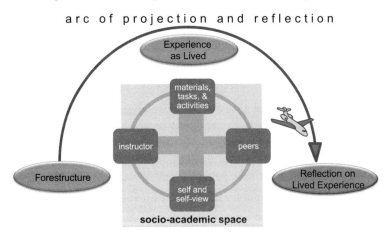

atmosphere as "close-knit" and likened it to a high school class—not in terms of ease of work but in terms of knowing everyone, having good discussions, and being a "student and not a number." Michelle found the atmosphere welcoming, and though she tended to be reserved in class, she said she did not "feel any uncomfortable situation . . . all students [were] trying to learn something." She went on to say that "classmates exchange ideas but they do not judge." For John, FYW was his favorite class, and "interaction made the class positive." For Luca, though she did not love the book that was the thematic focus of the class, she emphasized that she "really liked the girls [her classmates]" and felt they were "all in the same boat."

Discussions in the classroom setting seemed to be transactive, with many ideas moving around: "small class . . . can discuss more and try to get ideas from classmates and professor" (Kristen); "good thing to interact more with classmates" (Lora); "student discussions really interesting" (Crystal). Kristen noted that the professor, rather than seeming remote, was an active part of the class: "really into what he's talking about." As the second interview showed, this dynamic discussion-based atmosphere set the tone for the experience, but it was also sometimes seen as a source of pressure. For example, one participant noted

that interactions with peers were helpful for gaining new perspectives but that the small class size sometimes created a feeling of claustrophobia: "This class is small—I feel more pressure
from it."

Participants' conception of this socio-academic space was
further revealed through their comparison of FYW to other
classes they took in the same semester. Many participants
compared this class to "huge" lecture courses, where they had
little or no interaction with their professor and classmates. Ai
described this in the following terms:

> I know for freshman, we don't have that much small
> classes, but I think FYW is one of my small classes I have
> for my freshman year, and then it's more require me a
> lot of discussion. [But] I take an Econ and you don't need
> to respond, just sit there and listen to the professor's lec-
> ture . . . but for FYW I need to not only listening to profes-
> sor, it also require me thinking and then involving in the
> discussion so really pushing me learning stuff.

Ai's comments imply that in other classes, he could remain quiet
and just absorb the professor's lecture, a rather passive approach
to teaching and learning. Others such as Kristen, Han Gil,
Michelle, and John described their big lecture classes in similar
terms, and Yoono noted that the FYW gave "balance" to the rest
of his engineering classes, which were highly technical.

Participants acknowledged, however, that the FYW class
was more demanding than most of the other classes on their
schedule. Crystal could handle the quantitative aspects of her
business classes with relative ease, but she said FYW was "the
one I paid the most attention. Like [for] others, I could easily
follow the teacher, I could easily understand what I need to do
because some of them, like accounting, have a lot of math." Han
Gil said that the time he put into his assignments for the writing class far outweighed what he spent on work for his other
classes. While a number of participants emphasized that this
was the only course on their schedule that demanded significant

writing, Amy made mention of the fact that she did not really consider it a "writing" course; she said it was "different because I have so many, like, connections with this course. I have connections with the topic. It make me feel, like, it's kind of like a history course and also kind of like a research course, more about kind of an experience and a trip to the old times." Her other courses, by comparison, were seen as something "you have to take . . . other class, maybe international affairs, I just say 'Oh, yeah.' I definitely learn a lot. I know more about the international politics system and how states interact, but it's just not like an experience. It's not, like, oh, I took a trip to somewhere else."

One surprising finding from the second interview was that some participants mentioned peer review as a positive aspect of the class, which further underscored the importance of interactions with others in the socio-academic space. When asked to reflect on the overall class experience in the third interview, every participant commented on peer review as a significant— and positive—element of the experience. Part of the appeal of peer review was that it enabled the participants to engage more intimately with their classmates. As Han Gil said, peer review was the "best thing about the class," and he described his classmates as "really helpful . . . they always gave good comments." Amy, who had been paired with a classmate who was writing on a similar Holocaust-related research paper topic, "really liked" her partner for peer review and commented on how much effort her partner put into reviewing and "correcting" her writing and the closeness that developed between them based on the class project. Others commented on being amazed at how fortunate they were to have had peer reviewers who dedicated so much time to helping them. Crystal, for example, said she was surprised at how conscientious her peers were at commenting, and that one of her classmates had used the Microsoft Word comment function to give line-by-line comments on her draft. Luca said she got "lucky" with some reviewers and was amazed at how much help they gave her.

Another frequent comment was that peer reviewers tried to respond encouragingly to these L2 students' work: Yoono, for example, described peer review workshops in which classmates wrote letters to one another after reading assignment drafts. He commented that, though he knew his paper was "horrible," his classmates tried to be nice and say it "was not that bad." The caveat to this particular benefit was pointed out by several participants, however: One participant commented that her peers would say "You did well," but when she got her paper back she would realize "Uh oh that's not how the professor wanted it," and another said that even when his classmates gave him positive feedback, he felt his writing "could not reach the level the professor wants."

All of this is not to say that all participants mentioned getting nothing but positive feedback, but even when peer reviewers pointed out weaknesses in their writing, participants seemed to see this as an opportunity rather than as a critique that made them self-conscious or ashamed. Though Kristen was initially anxious about sharing her work, in the end she saw it as a positive thing; instead of criticizing her grammar, she knew her classmates would "correct [grammar] and help her." John described how it was not easy to have his weaknesses pointed out, but once he had a sense of what they were, he said he "started like focusing more on improving all that stuff and I think gradually my writing started going better and better so the grades were going up." Ai, like other participants, found having others read his paper very "useful" but added that reading his classmates' papers was beneficial as well "because we are all doing the same topic but we can see people choosing different images and have their own ideas." Lora liked the interaction and "learning how native Americans view questions or assignments." She also confessed that she appreciated reading her classmates' assignments and realizing that some of her American classmates were not as "good" as she expected. Some participants agreed, however, that it was a challenge to comment on their "American" peers' writing. Michelle described peer review as helpful, but acknowledged that "sometimes I was very jealous for American students . . . sometimes when I read [L1 peers' papers] I couldn't find anything to critique or analyze." And the following quote from Crystal captures both the struggle to contribute meaning-ful critiques and to even comprehend her peers' writing on cer-tain topics:

> Because their essays are good so it's hard for me to find some weak points. Like, I only, "Oh, it's good" but, like, I might just come up with some easy good point and then I say, "Oh, it's just good." But I don't know what a good point is. I just find it's hard to read American students' paper. They just have so many things new. Like, this time for the essay story, I did a peer review and for three American students. The two are okay because their topic is kind of common. One wrote for sports and another write for Katy Perry . . . and the other he wrote about space. It's just so hard. He discussed, like, a lot of, like, some people's view of it, like, opinions from very old time to now and there's so many new words in the space. It's awful.

This comment by Crystal taps into both gaps in content knowl-edge and the pressure to offer L1 peers meaningful critiques on their writing.

Course Theme versus Writing

By the third interview, discussion of the overall course theme was overshadowed by participants' work on individual research papers, but they still brought up the theme and how they came to understand it over the course of the semester. The first col-umn of Table 7.1 contains excerpts that capture participants' reflective comments on how the thematic content of the course changed their thinking.

These quotes indicate that most participants had gained a depth of understanding about the topic, not just in terms of generic description or factual background information, but some demonstrable ways of thinking about and engaging with the topic. Several participants, especially Amy and John, even

Table 7.1: End-of-the-Semester: Reflections on the Lived Experience

Pseudonym	Change in Thinking Based on Course Theme	Words to Describe the Lived Experience after FYW Class Ended		
Han Gil	"music is not entertainment . . . how lyrics and music have influenced people or culture or country [as focused on] lyrics, authenticity, culture"	Fun	Stressful	Meaningful
Crystal	"I think maybe a little bit better but, like, I still can't do the abstract one but for the thing more, like, close to our life, maybe it's easier. Like, you could have some guess about it because all the students' discussions, they have different type of images. They all have different tastes and they all choose different kind of image."	Challenging	Helpful	Involvement
Ai	"Before I took the class, I don't know that image can tell that much story but after that, I can see how image as powerful as a textbook . . . the picture is telling so many things so you just see them and then just interpret it different."	Content (satisfied)	Relief	Freshman (formative experience for first year)
John	"Every time I see a tweet, I think why did they post this, what do they want to say . . . I'm kind of into that social media world."	Enjoyable	Engaging	Innovating
Amy	"I actually didn't know much about the Jewish Holocaust, so right now if I heard something that is related to the Holocaust, I will always feel connected to that . . . like, I have a radar."	Impressive	Meaningful	Deep

Pseudonym	Change in Thinking Based on Course Theme	Words to Describe the Lived Experience after FYW Class Ended		
Lora	"Before I took this class, I thought architecture was only a project . . . but in the class I found out architecture's relationship to other disciplines."	Work hard	Thoughtful	Fulfill requirement
Michelle	At the beginning the theme seemed "easier" than the others; "before taking course, I just looked at whole things [images] not that small parts of the picture."	"More" challenging	Precious experience	"More" effort
Kristen	"We use sport or dance as a tool to investigating the problem in society or thing they represent, so kind of like go from surface to more deep."	Participating	Researching/ Reading	Brainstorming
Yoono	"Broadened my thinking . . . aspects from which we looked at food were so diverse . . . did not whatsoever expect to look at food as a form of study or form of history . . . "	Interactive	Challenging	Critical (thinking and analysis)
Luca	"To try to make us add something to the discourse community [of fan fiction]."	Fun	Relieving	Challenging

believed that this class cultivated in them an enduring interest and level of attentiveness toward the course theme. The table also lists the words participants used to describe the FYW experience after they finished the class and had submitted the final assignment. These words seem to encompass the challenge associated with the class, a challenge that became more "real" to them through the course of the semester as they tried to manage the heavy workload. At the same time they also capture the spirit of engagement ("involvement," "participation," "interactive," "fun," "enjoyable"), as well as a depth of thinking about the thematic content of the course ("critical," "meaningful," "impressive," "thoughtful," "deep," "precious").

As noted previously, during the first and second interviews, participants tended to discuss the overall course theme more frequently than the writing, but in the second half of semester, it was clear that writing began to take precedence; thus, in a way the topic became secondary or more likely to be linked through individual research project topics. Though reading dense scholarly texts for homework and keeping up with the general workload were characterized as challenges, the "big" writing assignments produced both the most stress and the most satisfaction upon completion. As a result of the shift toward "writing" in the second half of the semester, participants were far more likely to comment on how they felt their writing-related skills had improved; for example, John felt he developed a greater awareness of genre and structure, and Lora said that her vocabulary and reading skills improved. A number of participants mentioned changes in the way they approached research and integrating sources: "None of my sources came from Google and that's unlike my previous research . . . I learned how to research better [and] understood better the essence of going through databases rather than Google Scholar or like Google" (Yoono); "take time to do research" (Han Gil); "integrating scholars' quotations" (Lora); "researching topic helped evolve my thinking" (Kristen); "she [the professor] taught us how to do footnotes . . . when you can do footnotes, you can really add" (Amy).

Still other comments related to the development of ideas in writing. Michelle said she learned to think more critically, write a thesis, and draw a conclusion; she believed she was "building a strong foundation to develop as a writer." Ai learned to take a strategic approach to topic selection so that he could more easily build an argument into his writing, and Crystal indicated that she came to know what her "problems" were—explanation, clarification, and having a strong claim—though she was still uncertain about how to resolve them. These findings indicate an awareness of the characteristics of university-level writing in English even if they still have a hard time meeting these expectations.

Another notable element of participants' response to the writing expectations of the FYW class was the strategies they developed to manage these assignments. For Amy, meeting with the professor outside of class was imperative because "reading assignment prompt and comments not enough"; the secret was "figuring out what she wants." Crystal, Lora, Ai, Michelle, and Han Gil also discussed reaching out for support from the professor and other resources on campus, such as the writing center. One participant, however, expressed frustration that the professor "tells us to go to WC [writing center]" or visit office hours but that when the student did, he found that his grade was "always the same either way." For one participant, the secret was figuring what was really important and needed attention and not taking other tasks too seriously; for example, posting on the blog had been stressful for her, but she came to realize that "no one will read them" so in the end gave assignments like this less of her attention. John learned to dedicate time to a careful reading of the assignment prompt, look for models of that type of writing, and pay attention to feedback to improve future drafts. Both Ai and Michelle articulated the need for hard work to improve their chances for success: "I take this class really seriously compared to other" (Ai); "I tried to go to every class, every time . . . do all assignments on time [and] keep in touch with the professor." These comments convey both a determination to succeed and a strategic approach to positioning themselves for this success.

A Sense of Accomplishment

The final theme that emerged from the third interview—a sense of accomplishment—vividly encapsulated the entire participant experience. Table 7.2 outlines participants' reflection on finishing the class.

Table 7.2: Reflections on Finishing the Mainstream First-Year Writing Class

Pseudonym	Feeling on Last Day	Sense of Accomplishment	Advice for Peers
Han Gil	"Finally done . . . I feel happy."	"I felt like I actually went through this class . . . really thought I couldn't finish the research paper" (but did).	"It's better if you choose a course topic you like [rather than] pushing yourself to go through a whole semester with a topic you don't care about."
Crystal	"Felt a little sad [on last day] but more happy because this class is hard . . . 'Oh, I finally finished the class.'"	Wrote longest paper she had ever written and "made improvement on revision . . . you see the difference between first finished work [and think] 'Oh, I changed a lot.'"	"Really focus on professor himself and theme of class . . . choose something you don't need much background [for]."
Ai	"Sad to say goodbye to this group."	"I feel confident. I finished paper."	"Definitely find a topic you are passionate about . . . if you are not interested you will hate it and not have a good grade and won't have a happy FYW class memory."
John	"There was like some good aspects, like I don't have to go to class anymore, so that was kind of a relief. But at the same time, I was thinking, like, going back, like, to the whole year, and I was saying, like, I think that was the class that I enjoyed the most."	"The fact that I know I can write that much if I focus myself and put in the effort."	"If he [a friend] has a topic he is really passionate about, it would be really fun."
Amy	"I didn't think this class ends . . . this one is more like an experience."	"Proud."	"Know what the professor wants and really pick a topic that you're interested in."

Pseudonym	Feeling on Last Day	Sense of Accomplishment	Advice for Peers
Lora	"Relief" that it was done	Sense of accomplishment because reading and writing improved and "creative" ideas come more easily; can "explore through sources" and "bring a new idea to write about."	"Choose wisely and be prepared to work hard."
Michelle	"I felt free."	Felt "good" when during the last peer review session, her American classmates said: "We can't imagine how you are writing 12-pages paper in another language."	"Choose a topic he or she is interested in."
Kristen	Felt "relaxed" and "happy" and said, "Finally I can get a good sleep and I don't need to worry about this anymore."	"really proud . . . the longest paper I had ever written" (15 pages).	"[It is] not really hard but you have to work really hard;" "do everything on time and it's easy."
Yoono	"I felt kind of happy because we didn't have any more FYW class. It's always like relieving to finish a class, you know?"	"I actually felt proud of myself that I finished this class and that I managed to stick it out and do well 'cause a lot of people are, like, afraid of FYW, not a lot of people fancy it but I mean I worked hard and I did well on my papers."	"Dedicate time to doing the work and try your best to enjoy the class cause that's probably the only way you're going to stick through it."
Luca	"Sad because I really liked the professor."	"Felt a huge weight lifted off my shoulder."	"Think thoroughly if you really have the patience to only talk about one book."

Note: Excerpts in the table are a combination of participant's direct speech, as indicated using quotation marks, and description paraphrased by the researcher.

It is clear that that relief was a common feeling for participants when they finished the class, and that occasionally participants commented on feeling sad about saying goodbye to their professor and classmates. Participants' sense of accomplishment, as revealed by the quotes, often derived from their success on the major writing assignment, which serves as a reminder that—though the course theme had a clear influence on the experience—in the end it was the writing that seemed to carry the most weight. These quotes create a distinct impression that the experience was made meaningful as a result of the hard work participants put in.

The final column summarizes the "advice" each participant said they would give to a friend who was thinking about taking the class. This advice is clearly a reflection of what participants themselves went through during the course of the semester. Two major patterns emerged in the advice they would give: (1) choose a topic that is relevant and meaningful so as to sustain interest over the course of the semester and (2) be prepared to put in hard work. In terms of advice, some participants went on to give various strategies about how to manage the course better: "interact with professor . . . participate into the activities . . . be hard working even if you are not" (Lora); "try not to write like high school . . . try to think from American perspective . . . visit professor . . . try to do your best" (Han Gil); "use the resources available to help you . . . keep in touch with the professor" (Michelle); "be more open minded because you're going to listen different students and hearing their opinions . . . be really talkative because you need to be in the discussion . . . our class size only 15 students, if you don't speak in that class, other students will know and professor will notice that you're not actively participating in class" (Ai). These comments highlight the extent to which participants were aware of the course's expectations and committed to managing these strategically.

8

Reflecting from a Distance

Chapters 5–7 explored the "lived experience" of the ten L2 students during the semester in which they were enrolled in a mainstream first-year academic writing class at a U.S. university. As a follow up to the interviews conducted during participants' first year of study, I sought Institutional Review Board (IRB) approval to conduct interviews with the participants from the original study as most were entering their final semester of undergraduate study. All ten participants were invited to participate, and four responded to my email inviting them to meet with me again to share their experiences and reflections from a distance of three years. This chapter features highlights from interviews with Ai, John, and Lora, focusing on their characterization of their overall experience as a U.S. undergraduate student, their reflection on FYW and subsequent socio-academic experiences, their motivation to migrate transnationally for higher education, and the ways in which their past experiences are projecting them toward the future they envisioned for themselves, then and now.

Ai

Ai was the first to respond to my message for a follow-up interview; his message conveyed the same level of enthusiasm and generosity of spirit that he had displayed in the first set of interviews. Ai's hometown was Guangzhou, in the Canton Province of southeastern China. At the time of the follow-up interview, he was 22 years old and entering his final semester of undergraduate study with a double major in international business and information systems. During the interview, Ai spoke quickly and fluently in English, and his responses were peppered with vocabulary that showed the extent to which he had entered the discourse community of a U.S. undergraduate on the cusp of graduating and getting a job. The final interview with Ai was both a testament to the experiences he had created and to his sense of self—notably his determination to be self-actualized—within these experiences. Though Ai shared a great many things in this interview, I have selected several themes that illuminate these experiences for him: transformative experiences; his evolving self-view; socio-academic reflections; reflections on the decision to study in the United States; and plans for the future.

Transformative Experiences

Two particular experiences seemed to stand out in defining Ai's undergraduate life in the United States. First, he studied abroad twice: a summer in Paris, France, after his first year, and a semester abroad in London during his junior year. In addition to the other well-documented benefits of study abroad, Ai seemed to see study abroad as part of his *U.S.* academic experience because so many students at this university participate in study abroad programs. He also viewed study abroad as enhancing both his global outlook and his resume as he entered the job market: "I feel like international background and my culture aspect is really one of my strengths . . . I feel like that gave me the opportunity to leverage an understanding of the culture and distances between people."

Ai also considered his experience as both a member of and leader of a "business exclusive" fraternity on campus to be significant, saying, "I am really glad I joined that fraternity because I met lots of bright brothers and friends since then, and yeah, that kind of stepped out of my comfort zone, now I am fitting better you know, like, trying to meet more American people, making friends and just network with them." He considered his leadership experience in this fraternity as one of his greatest challenges and one of his greatest successes: "I guess one of my challenges, you know, just making my way up to the leadership role as an international student and, you know, managing a really diverse student body. We have a range of 80 members from different countries and also [the group is] really dynamic. . . . I feel like there's a lot of things happening and really, like, drama in a sense."

Evolving Self-View

Even in the earliest interviews I engaged in with Ai, it was clear that he was both determined and optimistic, and these characteristics were perhaps even more recognizable in the follow-up interview. On one level, he worked extremely hard and was proud of his accomplishments, particularly maintaining a GPA that qualified him not only for the dean's list but also for membership in an honor society for students ranked in the top 3 percent of their class. It also seemed that Ai was motivated by *measuring* his own success—both by his own yardstick and that of his peers. He described this not as "pressure" but said, "Yeah, that's my motivation, and also getting respect from my peers and also getting recognized by different organizations, like I got invitation to join honor society. I feel like those recognitions really give me the motivation to continue to improve myself."

The other side of this perspective for Ai was that he still had concerns about how he was perceived by others: "Definitely it does something, like draw me back still in my mind because I still care what people talk about me even though when I came to the United States, I have, like, fresh, you know, kind of like fresh cells because, people don't know about that much about my background unless I told those stories . . . You introduce yourself and try to be more positive, you want to, like, to be the best yourself." This is perhaps best reflected in the way he referred to his American persona; during the interview, he would sometimes refer to himself using his American nickname, something he said was part of a "brand" he was determined to project. Though he said his social life was spent "50/50" with American friends from his fraternity and Chinese friends, he seemed to be his truer self with the Chinese friends:

> So with American friends, I feel like that is the brunt of [English nickname] being more positive and being, like, smiling and just, like, energizing all the time. But with some close friends from hometown, they probably know the same kind of struggle that we face every day, like you judged by other people and you know that kind of more close friends. You talk more like your inner self feeling. Being with my Chinese group of friends, I [am] more true of me, I would say. But I still feel like I was wearing a mask to pretend a better version of me to my American friends, but I just want to say that being with my Chinese friends, I feel that I'm more comfortable, you know, just, like, hanging out, chatting with them.

A recurrent theme of my follow-up interview with Ai was his determination to write his own "story," and he viewed all of his experiences—positive and negative—as contributing to the story he wanted to write.

Socio-Academic Reflections

With the exception of his first semester EAP class, in which he earned an A–, Ai was proud to note that he had gotten As in FYW and the two required writing in the disciplines classes at the university. He attributed his success in part to "utilizing the resources" that the university provided but also recognized a growing sense of confidence in managing writing assignments: "Maybe the first time, when I first take an EAP or even my first or second assignment for [FYW] class, it was kind of still stressful and nervous like, 'Oh, can I do this?' like, kind of in that mind, but now I feel like, 'Yeah, I can do that.'" A similar level of confidence had grown when it came to classroom-based interactions. Ai recalled feeling intimidated during his first year if a class required participation as part of the grade; by the time he was a senior, he was still a bit nervous about speaking out during class but overall felt that was "an easy grade to get" and said, "I feel like I am more comfortable joining class with heavy class participation."

Similarly, to Ai, responding in either English or in Chinese—depending on the speaking context—felt "natural" to him, though he noted that when he went back to his hometown, his grandparents told him that his "tongue is changing." When reflecting on going back home, Ai also said that his friends from home said he has changed and become more "American-ized," though it was clear that Ai saw this more as a shedding of "labels." Though his friends remember him in a certain way—the way he was before he left for his high school exchange program in the United States—he said, "Now I am really comfortable speaking aloud and just, like, be who am I. I know in the past, even though we were in China, I have been thinking about all the labels, like what people think about me and stuff and I feel like now, I am really international. I have different international views . . . the study abroad experiences give me the horizon to see everything differently than students studying only in China."

Reflections on the Decision to Migrate Transnationally for Higher Education

In terms of his decision to study in the United States, it would seem Ai was not only happy with his decision but that he fulfilled his own goals for studying in the United States. For example, he succeeded academically and built a resume and "leveraged" contacts for future career opportunities while at the same time transforming from what he called "a little boy" to "a mature individual." Like the first set of interviews, he characterized this as part of his "journey," an idea he characterized quite visually: At the beginning, he said he felt his life had many paths, but as he progressed, he said, "They are narrowing down by becoming . . . one destination." Ai also repeatedly referred to his global outlook and his ability to understand diverse perspectives—a mindset he had cultivated as a result of his time studying abroad. In his initial description of the decision to study in the United States, he had talked about getting out of China and his hometown to expand his horizons. His success in this setting, I believe, was in large part driven by his attitude. When asked what advice he would give others considering studying abroad, his response reflected his own experience in very direct ways: "Think where you want to be . . . . Get involved in the community you are in . . . . Step out of comfort zone . . . . Don't get turned down when people judge you . . . . If you are holding a strong belief, then I feel like nothing is impossible . . . . Making more connection with different people that will be a great asset in the future." And by engaging fully and overcoming challenges, he believes, you can have "different stories to tell."

The Path Forward

It was apparent that Ai was working toward his future—and writing his own story—long before I met him for the first set of interviews. Much of the work he did as a student in the U.S. university centered on his self-actualization—that is, becoming who he wanted to be—and leveraging his opportunities for success. He chose to double major in international business and information systems to gain a "competitive advantage" by having a global perspective while at the same time having a technical skill set. It was clear to me throughout the follow-up interview that Ai had been working to package his skills and market himself in the workforce; in fact, some of his responses to my questions felt like job interview responses at times—though this in no way made his responses ring false. Because of Ai's awareness of what his peers were planning and accomplishing, he felt a certain motivation to cultivate his own advantage as he entered the workforce. He said he wanted to get a job and stay in the United States for the next five to ten years but expects he will eventually return to China because that is where his "roots" are. Just before our interview, Ai had been offered a position with the organization Teach for America (TFA) in San Jose, California, and he was leaning toward accepting that position. Though teaching was not in his plans, he thought that being in the "technology hub" of Silicon Valley would be relevant for his degree in infosystems and offer him a new set of contacts for networking. He also emphasized the fact that he was interested in education because he "came to the U.S. to pursue an education," and he thought that teaching for TFA, whose "mission is helping lower community student to fill the gap," would help him add to his own "story."

John

Like Ai, John also readily agreed to a follow-up interview and, at 22, was entering the final semester of undergraduate study in the United States. When asked his hometown at the beginning of the interview, I was struck by the fact that John said "DC," rather that the hometown in Ecuador he had named in our first interview three years before. John was completing his degree in the business school, with a double major in international business and marketing. Though I had not seen John in several years and he had clearly grown up in the intervening years, as soon as he started speaking, I was brought back to his manner of speaking. At the point of the final interview, he was living in an apartment off campus, working an internship, and trying to finish up some required courses to graduate on time.

Transformative Experiences

John described his junior year as one where he went through "a bit of a stumble." At the very last moment, a close friend that he intended to room with decided to take a leave of absence from the university. He was randomly assigned a roommate that was not a good fit, and everything seemed to fall apart from there: "Sometimes if you're not in the right environment, it's really easy to fall into a comatose state, like, whatever, into the whole purpose of why you are here." Eventually, he found his place again and even came to appreciate the struggles he had gone through, telling me, "I think that was kind of worth mentioning cause it really affected me in a way; but in a way it helped me in retrospective because now every time I feel like I'm down for 2 or 3 days, it's like, 'You're not going to let that fall semester junior year happen, like, get it together, focus, like, what are you doing here?'"

I would say that a second key transformation during John's undergraduate life was the reorientation of his life away from campus and into the wider city, as a result of a move to an apartment off campus and an internship at a local start-up. He described his early relationships at the university as including a wide circle of international students who "meshed together" but then over time "everybody spreads out" and the circle becomes much smaller. Living off campus, according to John, "gets you off that university grid in a way." Though certain connections are lost—and he no longer lives in the "protected" space of dorm life—he sees clear benefits to living off campus and being independent, including more "professionalism . . . another view towards the future," which in turn contributes to a greater sense of self-sufficiency and what he called "real stuff." Part of his life off campus also involved an internship working in the sales and marketing unit of a local company. John admitted that he did not immediately pursue such internships, even though the business school had given students early opportunities, and that it was "social pressure" that finally motivated him—in other words, seeing his peers land impressive internships or jobs. He seemed pleased he found an internship that enabled him to tap his interest in marketing and his ability to speak Spanish and thought it could offer some advantage over the native English speakers he might compete against in the marketplace.

Evolving Self-View

During the first set of interviews, John described himself as a "planner," which provided him a sense of security. This characteristic remained evident when he reflected on his experiences as a senior; if anything, he said, his tendency to plan had gotten "more complex . . . when I've checked off all of them [items on his list] or most of them, I'm like, 'Alright today was really productive even though you didn't do anything from class, but the way of success is like those small victories; you can live on your own, you can survive.'" This comment speaks to his overall approach to managing his life and also offers insights into how he defines success: Though he said it was easy to get caught up in feeling that the goal is the "diploma" and that everything is "defined by grades," to him it was equally important to recognize the value of all of the other learning that goes on. As he said: "I think it's more by what you learned, not even in class or what did you learn in class but around being in a group of people, like group projects or people that you met in class or you met afterwards and you're, like, friends with them—that kind of interactions, I think, is something that is a well-defined success."

Similar to Ai, John talked about who he felt closest to, or shared his real self with. He said he had always been reluctant to share his personal feelings with his family, perhaps because "growing up, like, we're four brothers. We were constantly fighting, like, who has upper hand to bully the other one . . . so I think every time you say anything, like, coming from the heart or sharing a problem, even with my parents, it's like sharing a weakness so that's something they can pin on you." His girlfriend, an Ecuadorian international student at another local university, was one person with whom John shared his true feelings. Though he had good friends who were not Spanish speakers, he also characterized his relationships with a close-knit group of Spanish-speaking peers as naturally open, noting that "in Spanish it feels more like it just blurts out sometimes."

Socio-Academic Reflections

When asked what he remembered about the first-year writing class experience, unlike Ai—who largely focused on his growing confidence as a writer without mentioning the course content—John noted that the course theme had indeed shaped his later experiences: "I was writing about something I liked. . . . I'm doing marketing, like, I think that class kind of took an important turn into my academics because I thought I feel like I am good for this, like, maybe I should look into marketing . . . It was, like, totally useful." He also reflected sheepishly on his performance in that class; though he characterized himself as a planner even then, it seems that he felt he did not always follow through on his intentions. These days, not only is he better at following through with his plans but he also has the confidence to know he can manage even heavy writing assignments. He gave an example of a 2,500-word paper he had recently been assigned, saying, "I did it in six hours and usually, like back in the day, it would take a week or so to do, so it was, like, I think it shows the progress, the way I feel more comfortable writing in English that I don't take so many stops like translating or using a thesaurus." In reflecting on how he has changed as a writer, he felt more confident not only as a writer, but as a writer who had a "style" (voice) and a "point of view."

Similar to Ai, his perspective on classroom participation had also evolved. Some of this was natural and some was a deliberate effort to become more "professional" and engage more in class. Though he was not wholly satisfied, he thought he had "made some strides about it, a little bit late, but better late than never." John related a particular anecdote about a time he felt he garnered "high esteem"—not to mention a strong letter of recommendation—from his professor because of a leadership role he had taken on in a group project in the business school, which involved a "real client" the group had to develop a marketing plan for. As a senior, John characterized his approach to class participation not as "obvious" participation—for example, raising his hand or engaging in debate in class—but rather as "silent leadership" where he might carry the load of the project and be recognized for this after the fact. For him this was an example of a "meaningful" experience because, as he said: "It has developed . . . my involvement and how I interact with a group itself in college."

In terms of his overall English language use, John said the fact that he was immersed in an internship situation in which only "plain English"—with no opportunity for Spanish—was used was of benefit to him:

> [It] helped me a lot with my accent, like, to get out of that shell of self-consciousness a bit but still sometimes, like,

I say to my friends, I woke up without English and my accent is terrible. I cannot find the words to say, like, to speak, English. When I am writing, I'm just making the silliest mistakes in verbs like if the sentence is present, I just put the verbs in past—stuff like that. But I think that just comes with the baggage of not being a native speaker, English speaker. But in the end, I feel like I improve a lot, like, I haven't felt so self-conscious especially in language like business jargon, for example in my job. It's been really developed since I first came and I think it also shows on my papers.

Reflections on the Decision to Migrate Transnationally for Higher Education

Also similar to Ai, there was a consistency in how John described his motivation to study abroad during his first year of study and how he conveyed it during the follow-up interview. Perhaps the most encapsulating statement John made about the decision to pursue an undergraduate degree in the U.S. was as follows: "I think it's been worth every penny, like, every effort I had, like, back then since the moment I thought, 'I'm going out.'" John has even encouraged his brothers to follow a similar path, and he had some particularly thoughtful reflections about what would have happened if he had not gone abroad:

> We [he and his roommates] sometimes stay up till 5:00 in the morning just talking, talking about life and we were thinking, what would you do right now, like, your state of mind will be back in high school? . . . But I think I've done a pretty good job in getting through that growth process pretty well, and I think I am much more mature person back from three years, like, professional, academic, socially.

He goes on to describe the people he knows who have stayed in Ecuador as "permanently high school state," and, although it is sometimes easier to stay where you are known and comfortable, he clearly advocates for leaving that secure space. When considering going abroad for a higher education, he would advise others as follows: "If you think you want to do it, yes do it. There is no shame going back after a semester or a year if you didn't like it, but I think you get so much out of it, like, just trying to prove yourself. So it's really an experience that's worth a shot if you have the opportunity." At the same time, he warned of the danger of losing oneself in the new environment, stressing the importance of getting one's "moral compass" or "inner rules set in stone." This is part of what I admired about Ai as well: Even though they both grew and changed in powerful ways, they did not lose sight of who they were in the experience. I say this not only because they said it to me but because they demonstrated this "truth" consistently through every interview.

The Path Forward

John's future path was not as "narrow" as Ai's, and he admitted to having thoughts of going back home as he saw his friends and family putting down more roots in Ecuador. But as he entered his last semester of study, he felt "set in DC" and said it "matches him well" and "I feel like I'm home here." Interestingly, the same motivation that caused him to want to "go out" from Ecuador when he was young was making him want to "stay" in the city he is currently living in: "I have so much benefits being here, like, there are so many advantages to get. Like, there is no point of comparison and I think that motivation, like, right now that I feel like your visa is expiring, go get a job or you're going to get sent back. I think it kind of feels like the same spark, like, you need to get same motivation, get the same fire from back in the day to stay." But he still admitted to feeling torn, saying, "Either way there is a cultural distance because you've been missing the four years there or you spent the four years here. So you feel kind of like you are in no man land in a way so it's kind of hard especially, like, if you don't have a job offer or you don't have a job lined up for after graduation, you really feel like, 'What are you doing?' Should you just go back home? Will people think less of you?" Despite such thoughts, John is determined to get an internship or a job to be "independent" and self-sustaining while preparing to go to graduate school for an MBA, possibly pursuing the initial interest he conveyed during the first interview three years ago: sports management. Though John had a tentative sense of his future, it was clear he was still negotiating what it might look like—and trying to get through his final semester of study.

Lora

Perhaps the most surprising and interesting of my follow-up interviews was the one with Lora, who was a somewhat reticent though thoughtful participant in the early round of interviews. Though Ai and John looked the same when we met for the follow-up interview, just perhaps a bit more mature, Lora, a 22-year-old from inner Mongolia, came in with dyed blond hair that reflected a distinct and confident personal style. My first impression was that she had discovered—and was happy to display—who she was. Though her father had suggested that she study business or economics, she said to herself, "I can't do this—I hate it" and eventually followed her own interest, majoring in interior architecture and design. As a child, she had liked drawing but decided that she wanted to "do something I can apply" that "people can actually use [though] it also has aesthetic beauty." The experiences that Lora reflected on fell into similar categories to the other participants in the follow-up interviews, and hence are organized around similar themes, but at the same time reflect her unique and particularized voice and perspective.

Transformative Experiences

For Lora, I would say that two main experiences helped define her undergraduate life. First, as previously mentioned, Lora made a decision to follow her own interest in deciding her major, rather than adhering to the more pragmatic path her parents had expected for her (business or economics). She had always liked drawing and had an interest in architecture. Her path became clear when a career advisor took her on a tour of the interior design program, where she immediately felt right at home, thinking, "Oh my god, this is so amazing. It's, like, exactly what I want to do." She thus decided to major in interior design. It was clear that her experience in the small, intense, and rather insular interior design program has had a profound influence on her. For example, the work was intense but she loved it; she developed friendships and interpersonal coping skills as a result of "being stuck with [classmates] for six hours a day" in studio classes; she developed professional competencies as a result of close and direct relationships with her professors and an internship in a local design showroom.

The second experience that shaped Lora's undergraduate life was the fact that she joined an Asian sorority during her sophomore year. Her social life centered on this group, and she felt both welcomed and well supported in this community, saying "I feel like to belong to them . . . they are super nice and I really love them . . . nobody judges each other." Though by her senior year, she had mild regrets that she had spent so much time in the sorority instead of "put[ting] academic first," it was clear that she felt she had a home in that community. And though the sorority was Asian, Lora described it as extremely diverse, comprised of Asians and Asian Americans from a variety of backgrounds. According to Lora, this forced her to speak English more often, which was clearly important to her because as she stated in her follow-up interview, "Why am I coming here if I'm just talking to Chinese people all the time?" Being a member of this Asian sorority also enabled her to establish a balanced life between what she called "pure American and Chinese international community." Having said that, because she became so embedded in her field of study and moved off campus into a studio apartment as an upperclass student, she engaged less with her sorority peers and felt even more remote from the community of Chinese international students ("so far away from that world now").

Evolving Self-View

In my early interviews with Lora, she came across as self-restrained and reflective, though a little uncertain of her place.

By the time of the follow-up interview, when she was entering her final semester of study, I would describe her as being more centered yet at the same time more open. Similar to Ai, I would say she had self-actualized but on very different terms. She had followed her own interests, identified her own communities and situated herself fully within them, and was not afraid of being who she was. Part of this process involved negotiation; for example, when she first started at the university she said it was "hard to fit in as an international student." She was from China, but not from the big cities that many other students came from; she was from inner Mongolia, which many Americans confused with Mongolia. However, as Ai and John also admitted, when she was around some of her peers—in her case Chinese international students—she felt a sense of comparative pressure: "Sometimes I feel like they have really high grades. I feel that even though I do the best I can, I'm not as good as them."

However, the challenges she faced taught her "to become a better person" and to be selective and deliberate about who she wanted to spend time with and confide in. Her main confidants were her sorority sisters and her interior design classmates, to whom she opened up after collaborating on class projects. But there was almost a process of vetting involved as well—that is, she would not spend her time on relationships that did not suit her; as she said, "I feel like most people I talk to are the 'right' people already because I feel like this person is to my standard," and if people are not "morally nice, like, I just stop talking to this person or don't hang out if I don't have to." At the same time, she had to become resilient in response to people back home who told her "You're too Americanized." She even described a heartbreaking story of a fight that she had had with her parents in these terms:

> That's kind of the main reason we are arguing. I am not a bad person just because I have blonde hair. I still work hard, I do everything I can, I do my best about my school and working and everything. They are just like, "What kind of person have you become—you have blonde

hair now. It's not natural. How can you see your grand-parents? How can I bring you to your great grandparents or how can you see my friends?" I was like, "I don't care about your friends. I'm not even going to see them when I go back. I'm going to be exhausted. I only stay a week. Why do I care about them? Even if I see them, it's my life." Why would I change myself only because of other's opinions? They just don't understand—other people's opinions are really important. People judge you so you should be more careful about what you like or how you behave. I'm like, I'm just being myself. I'm not hurting people.

Socio-Academic Reflections

When asked to reflect back on her experience in the first-year writing class, her memory was largely colored by other things happening in her life—that is, stress from outside of the class-room. She said, "I feel if I was in a better condition [during the FYW semester] I could focus more." Lora did not do as well as she hoped in that class and ended up asking her professor to submit a "repeat" grade for her. She retook the FYW class during her sophomore year, this time with a film noir theme, and found it to be a positive experience. She "learned more how to study" by that time and also sought out the professor, something she had been hesitant to do during her first year: "Before I was kind of scared, like, 'Should I email him? Is he going to hate me if I email him too much?' but, like, after that, I emailed him as much as I can." Once Lora figured out the study approach that worked best for writing, she started doing much better and was particularly proud of the grade she earned in a writing-intensive art history class. Like Ai and John, Lora seemed to be a more confident writer and had matured in her approach to writing assignments. For example, instead of "writing right before the deadline," she started "turning in really early or write several drafts," seeking feedback from the writing center, the professor, or her sorority sisters. She also spoke of improvements in grammar and structure but more importantly, she had begun to develop her own voice as a writer—not just to "pull out facts" like she used to do: "Now I think I know how to write more critical, with critical thinking, and give my opinion."

In terms of her classroom personality and interaction in socio-academic contexts, Lora's experience was influenced by the nature of the interior design curriculum. Because many classes were "studio" classes, she was thrown into an environment where she had to work closely with a small group of classmates: "We are just familiar with each other because we take all the same classes together and spend so much time." She also said that in her department, it was both easy and natural to speak to professors very directly and that "the professor knows who we all are." In classes outside of her major, however, her participation depended on how engaged and prepared she felt. She seemed particularly interested in a philosophy class she was taking and said that she spoke a lot in that class, but in classes where the reading was heavy or the material was new, she tended to speak up less and concentrate on taking notes.

Reflections on the Decision to Migrate Transnationally for Higher Education

Very much like Ai and John, Lora characterized the decision to pursue an undergraduate degree in the United States as "the best decision I made in my life." She talked about feeling that she belonged because "people are more open and acceptable and I can have my own voice here"—especially in comparison to life in China, where she described the conformity as stifling:

> In China, the general environment, it's like everyone has to do the same thing and follow the same rule and, like, at a certain age, you need to get married, you need to go to grad school, or do this, do that. Family or parents expect you to do what the society expects you to do. I think here everybody just do what they want as long as not hurting other people and I feel like it makes me more comfortable to live here, and I feel like I'm happier here.

According to Lora, studying in the U.S. made her grow up, open up, and learn to be less judgmental of others. She perceived her high school friends who remained in China as living in a "bubble," emphasizing that either they had not changed at all or that—if they changed—it was still within the bubble. Much like John, she said, "I feel like they are still high school kids. . . . It's not bad what they are, it's just different from me, I guess." Studying abroad and meeting "friends from every culture" also allowed Lora exposure to a great deal of diversity, bring her into a global, cosmopolitan sphere similar to what Ai described.

The Path Forward

Like Ai and John, Lora was not interested in returning to her home country upon graduation. There was no doubt she felt that life in the U.S. suited her more, and she said, "I wish I could live here permanently if I could." Her top choice after graduating was entering a graduate program for architecture, and at the time of our follow-up interview, she was in the midst of applying to a number of Master's programs in the United States. If that does not work out—or, as she said, "If nobody wants me"—she hopes to find a job in the U.S. There was clarity in the forward path that Lora articulated but, at the same time, it had a sad resonance. She said she wanted to live in the U.S. because she felt she belonged but also because she feels "like my personality or the way I live can't fit in the Chinese society any more . . . I feel like if I go back, the society won't accept me."

Nonetheless, she would advise others considering pursuing a degree in the U.S. to blaze their own path like she did: "I would say do what you like the most. Don't do something because someone has expectation for you. Do what you really like and are passionate about," she said, because putting your time and energy into what you love can help you "contribute to society" and be "happier." She also advised seeing the world, being independent financially, and the importance of staying true to yourself, a thought that was echoed by John and Ai. Lora framed it succinctly and beautifully: "Be nice to people. Don't be arrogant. Listen to other people but you also need to speak your own opinion when it needs to."

Reflections on Reflections

In all honesty, it was amazing to speak with these participants again as they headed into their final semester of study at the U.S. university. Several broad themes emerged from these follow-up interviews, which I will sketch here but are certainly worthy of deeper analysis later. In all three of these cases, participants expressed absolute certainty that the decision to study abroad was the right one for them—that they changed in positive ways through negotiating new and sometimes challenging situations while simultaneously cultivating and maintaining a sense of self and integrity that was not compromised in the process. Their "centeredness" and the way they stayed true to themselves was an inspiration to me. A great deal of what transformed them was the "arc" of their experience over time, and the experiences they seemed to consider transformative were often linked to the communities they engaged with—curricular, co-curricular, social, and even professional. They narrowed their communities based on their understanding of themselves and their interests, in some cases moving away from the broad community they had engaged with in their first year of study.

While each of them found their place in the U.S. higher educational context and had no regrets about the decision to study abroad, in their own way they each conveyed a tension with "home" or with the parallel life they may have had if they had remained in their home country rather than coming abroad. In fact, independently from one another, they all implied that their high school friends were somehow "stuck" because they did not get out of that environment. The advice they would give to others considering migrating transnationally for higher education is testament to this: Follow your path. Open yourself up. Even if you fail, it is worth it. To me, this did not come across as clichéd advice because I had met with these students four times and knew they had *lived* these words. This was their truth, rendered consistently in their description of their experiences and their interpretation of themselves within these experiences.

On a socio-academic level, perhaps the most significant development was participants' feeling that they were more confident and proactive writers. Not only were they able to manage longer and more complex writing assignments better and take deliberate advantage of supporting resources on campus (writing center, professor, peers), but they all emphasized growing into their own "voice" as writers. In other words, they recognized where they had begun—particularly during the FYW course—and could now articulate both practical differences in their approach to writing and qualitative differences in developing a strong point of view as writers. In classroom contexts, these participants gained confidence but in some ways remained how they were during their FYW class, for example not necessarily being overly active in class but participating in smaller ways where it counted more. All three also clearly developed a conversational fluency in English that seemed natural, though in some cases they revealed that their true selves came through more when they were speaking their native language with their peers. These follow-up interviews remind us that the "arc of projection and reflection" is ongoing, and they validate the value of a hermeneutic phenomenological research approach using a socio-academic space model.

9

Key Themes and Broad Conclusions

The goal of this chapter is to link the findings of the study—the socio-academic experiences described and interpreted in Chapters 5 through 8—to key themes and to discuss their implications in light of existing literature. An influential framework for this study was the continuing trend of transnational mobility for higher education. Individual participants' backgrounds and motivations to study abroad, which are considered part of their "forestructure" in the socio-academic model, were elucidated in Chapter 3. This chapter focuses on how this research enhances our understanding of internationalization at an institutional and classroom level and what we can learn from orienting ourselves to the specific experience of L2 students in our FYW classes— and more broadly in our campus classrooms and communities.

A Return to the Literature: Internationalization of Higher Education

Motivation to Pursue Higher Education Abroad

Situating participants' experiences in the context of the internationalization of higher education provided an opportunity to take an aerial view of this phenomenon and to understand how participants were motivated to cross borders for higher education. These interviews explored participants' sociocultural histories and contexts for migration, and the findings add dimension to the literature on the internationalization of higher education, whose existing research base tends to focus on broad trends in global student flows (American Council on Education, 2012; NAFSA, 2016) and rationales and strategies for internationalization (Altbach & Knight, 2007; Brustein, 2007; Hayward, 2000; Qiang, 2003). Participants in this study are testament to global mobility trends, yet they are not merely numbers or statistics; rather they are individuals whose experiences have been shaped by their sociocultural histories, who have unique visions and voices when discussing their experiences and goals. Thus, an important implication of this research is that its findings challenge our status quo attitudes about "who" these international students are and how they are able to negotiate being a part of our socio-academic communities.

The first relevant point in this regard was the sheer diversity evident among the participants in this study. Though all participants met the criteria for the study, and all were considered L2 international students, they were not all products of similar educational environments, even those coming from the same country; in fact, only three participants in this study came from what would be called a traditional school setting in their home country. Nor did these participants necessarily come from monolingual, monocultural backgrounds; in some cases, they spoke the language of their home community and studied English as a foreign language in school, but several of the participants studied or spoke two or three languages with fluency. Participants also had varied and, in some cases, extensive opportunities for foreign travel, though my overall impression was that they likely came from fairly privileged socio-economic backgrounds. Some had even studied or participated in educational programs abroad, and many—though not all—participants had visited the United States prior to coming here for university. Even for participants with limited experience in transcultural, translingual settings, there was a sense of awareness and openness toward global mobility.

The diverse profiles identified in this study hint at what Rizvi (2005) called a new "cosmopolitan" dimension of global mobility: The background of participants in this study present a more "dynamic view of cultural identity" (p. 334), whereby students can inhabit any number of cultural or linguistic spaces and are not solely defined by their home country's culture or language. This heterogeneity also speaks to Kell and Vogl (2008) and Dervin's (2011) claim that research needs to take into account these new aspects of culture and mobility in a global society and highlights the danger of making assumptions based on superficial characteristics and the stigmatizing potential of labels (Canagarajah, 2002, 2006). If we fail to explore the "politics of difference" (Lobnibe, 2009) or focus our understandings on enrollment trends and stereotypical characterizations of cultures or languages, as is often prevalent in the literature (Heng, 2016), we lose an opportunity to develop the global understandings that transnational migration for higher education should, by definition, invite.

Despite the diversity evident among study participants—and the heterogeneity assumed among the million plus international students who studied in the United States in 2015–16 (Institute for International Education, 2016)—this study had phenomenological intent, which meant that its major goal was to identify the common features that undergirded the experience for all participants. Findings about participants' context for mobility clearly highlighted global interconnectedness, as discussed in the literature, in several different ways. First, the impetus for the internationalization of higher education is often linked to the dynamic interplay of global forces in our society (American Council on Education, 2012; Brustein, 2007; Hunter et al., 2006), and interviews indicated the extent to which participants and their families had been implicated in this global dynamic: In every case, families and often participants themselves had had transnational experiences, and each participant described the role that these sociocultural experiences played in their motivation to study abroad. Participants also framed the decision to study abroad in terms of the perception of benefit from a U.S. education and in terms of what they perceived as constraints within their home country—for example, lower-quality higher education or limited job opportunities if they attended a university in their home country. This aligns with what the literature calls the push-pull motivation for study abroad (Altbach, 2004; Chirkov et al., 2007; Lee, 2008; Mazzarol & Soutar, 2002). Such motivations are frequently tied to a desire for practical opportunities, such as seeking a higher-quality education for increased employment prospects after graduation.

However, though these participants certainly explained their motivations for studying in the U.S. in these ways, for example describing constraints in their home countries' higher education or opportunities to be gained by pursuing a degree abroad, it was surprising to note the various ways participants articulated motivations that went beyond the traditional push-pull categories. Participants frequently talked about deeper motivations such as "broadening horizons," "seeing the world," and "becoming independent," reflecting what I would call a quest for self-actualization. This finding maps with Bodycott's (2009) research on how motivations for study abroad differed between Chinese parents and their children. Parents' motivations were related to practical constraints and opportunities, much like the traditional push-pull categories, but the students sampled were motivated more by the perceived quality of a U.S. degree and a personal desire to have international and intercultural experiences. For some of my participants, this more personal motivation engendered a certain autonomy in their approach to studying in the United States: Approximately half the students initiated the idea to study abroad themselves, and several of them went to great lengths to conduct research and prepare for their own study abroad experience.

The fact that so many participants' responses conveyed self-actualization as a motivation to study abroad must be interpreted though the lens of their family backgrounds, however. As noted in Chapter 2, only a handful of participants mentioned their family's socio-economic status, but it was clear that they came from financially secure backgrounds. In other words, participants' families had the means and the willingness to invest in their educations, and the cost of higher education did not appear to limit their options. In fact, many of the participants researched and applied to relatively high-ranking, East Coast private colleges and universities, with several students applying to more than 10 institutions and touring campuses during their summer breaks. The participants in this particular setting align with what Choudaha, Orosz, and Chang (2012) would call the new profile of international students, fitting into the categories of "explorers" and "highfliers." Both explorers and highfliers are financially well supported, although explorers tend to have less academic preparation than highfliers. The important commonality to note in this regard is that the participants in this study, though diverse in many ways, operated from a position of socio-economic security and took a relatively opportunistic approach to study abroad.

Another important point to consider in exploring participants' motivation and opportunity to study abroad was that, though they had a stated goal of self-actualization and framed the decision to study abroad more as opportunity than pressure, most indirectly indicated what could be called an entrepreneurial agenda, which links back to the broader internationalization context. A number of participants were in the business school, with several in the international affairs program, and one was in engineering; participants who were in the arts and sciences college seemed to be pursuing social science rather than humanities degrees. The motivation to pursue such practical fields may in part be attributed to their parents. For example, a number of participants were pursuing a major that was similar to their parents' professional field, and a number of participants indicated that their parents were themselves entrepreneurs. One participant, Lora, spent much of her first year fighting against her parents' expectation that she major in economics or business, rather than the design-related field she was truly interested in. The fact that international students tend to major in practical fields matches the Institute of International Education's (2016) *Open Doors* data on international students' fields of study, which shows that more than 60 percent of international students were seeking degrees in engineering, business, math/computer science, or social science. Less than 2 percent were pursuing degrees in the humanities.

Though participants' career paths were not always clear, many pictured themselves working in an international business—or international organization—context. This is an interesting "flipped" perspective on what Stromquist (2007) considered the institutional motivation to internationalize—a push toward marketable skills in the global economy—as well as Altbach and Knight's (2007) emphasis on the market orientation of the internationalization agenda. It seemed that the participants themselves were consumers in the U.S. higher education marketplace and that they were linking an education abroad to a set of applicable outcomes, despite the rhetoric of self-actualization. Hence, a conclusion I would like to draw from this study is that participants were operating from a position of strategic awareness in deciding to study in the United States, in accessing information about schools and programs, and in evaluating options for themselves. This finding has particular implications as the global marketplace for international students becomes increasingly competitive and internationalization agendas are strategically activated at national, sector, and institutional levels (Engel & Siczek, 2017).

The picture that emerged from these interviews highlights both the diversity and the commonality of these participants' transnational migration experiences and helps us examine the assumptions that often characterize our perceptions of international students (Heng, 2016; Lobnibe, 2009). The diversity evident among the study participants serves as a reminder that as policymakers and educators we need to unpack the profile of our international student populations. Just because they are all classified as "international" or "second language" or attend the university on a student visa, it does not mean they are uniform in their experiences or needs (Ferris, 2009). The common elements of their experience, those that shaped their context for mobility, offer us additional insights into what influences the particular phenomenon of pursuing a higher education abroad. Further, some of the main themes that emerged from participants' narrative accounts of their motivation to pursue higher education abroad—including access to global experiences, familial and financial support, and a sense of individual autonomy—reflect Rizvi's (2005) point about the international students becoming increasingly cosmopolitan, "underpinned by a more dynamic view of cultural identity that emerges out of the conditions of global interculturality; and of critical engagement with ideas and images that circulate around the world" (p. 334).

Institutional-Level Internationalization

In terms of global flows and enrollment trends, the literature on the internationalization of higher education tends to present international students as commodities in the global education marketplace (Altbach & Knight, 2007; Brennan & Dellow, 2013; Dolby & Rahman, 2008), and there was no doubt that participants in this study were part of the university's agenda to enroll more revenue-generating students. Similar to the literature, there was also evidence of an institutional focus on the recruitment of international students from the Pacific Rim (Stromquist, 2007) and from burgeoning middle-class backgrounds around the world (Fischer, 2011). These enrollments also fell in line with university-level strategic plans that aim to increase international student enrollments and diversify the student body, reinforcing Hall's (2014) point that "multilingualism is the mainstream" (p. 31) in U.S. higher education. The question then becomes: To what extent are colleges and universities orienting themselves to this diversity?

As emphasized previously, on an institutional level, the enrollment of international students is often highlighted as evidence of a school's commitment to global engagement, as articulated in mission statements and other institutional documents, yet the present study supports the contention that most institutions are only marginally internationalized when it comes to teaching and learning (Caruana, 2010; Jones & Killick, 2007; Kreber, 2009; Leask, 2001). To support this point, I would like to consider the thematic content of the required FYW course, both the course themes selected by my participants and the course themes they chose not to select. Despite a marked increase in the number of culturally and linguistically diverse students in these required classes, the majority of themes offered were American—or Western—in their orientation, and participants tended to choose themes that were somewhat more generic; hence, we see participants choosing courses about social media, music, or images as text, rather than courses about U.S. politics, Western film, or African-American rhetorics or poetics. Some participants even studiously avoided selecting any course that had an American reference in its title, for fear that they would lack the cultural knowledge base from which to understand it. Other participants described feeling lost or disconnected when they lacked the historical or cultural context for some point of discussion in the class, even though they had chosen class topics they had thought were less culture-bound. Thus, though the themes of the FYW courses are intended to be socially and intellectually meaningful to students, the options were often limited to Western themes and constructs and did not engage with what Van Gyn et al. (2009) would call "diverse sources and contexts of knowledge" (p. 26). This speaks to the gap between the big-picture rhetoric and policies of the institution and the on-the-ground reality for L2 students in classroom settings.

Further, despite this institutional reality, much of the research on international students takes the form of acculturation studies—in other words, how well these "foreign" students adjust to existing educational frameworks. In the literature on the international student experience in U.S. higher education, the primary trends that emerged were:

- adjustment
- English language proficiency
- academic adjustment
- cross-cultural interactions

Though this study was directed at a particular socio-academic experience, participants certainly discussed elements external to the class that provided insight into their overall experience in the U.S. university. In interview data, there was no strong evidence of acculturation challenges; most participants conveyed a strong network of peers and frequent contact with family and friends from home. Though there were a few individual examples of anxiety coming into the university or of homesickness, by the second semester—when these interviews took place—participants seemed to have adapted relatively well to the new setting. Though some participants acknowledged having a hard time making American friends, they seemed to think that domestic students were friendly and welcoming to them, at least on a superficial level.

Similar to existing research, English language proficiency featured prominently for most participants; for some, there was a general perception of language deficiency or of being an L2 speaker in an L1 world, but most examples of language difficulty were framed situationally—a point that will be explored in greater depth later in this chapter. In terms of academic adjustment, similar to the existing literature, this topic was brought up fairly frequently in interviews. However, the existing research presents a picture of an unprepared, naïve student who has little sense of the classroom realities of U.S. colleges and universities, whereas these participants did not seem at all unaware of the expectations or the pedagogical approach of the class. In fact, before they even arrived at the university, most participants had an accurate picture of what the U.S. college classroom was like based on American movies and TV and on information gained through family and peer networks.

Despite having a fairly accurate picture of what to expect in a U.S. college classroom, language proficiency and lack of experience with academic writing naturally impacted their academic adjustment, particularly for participants who had come from more monolingual backgrounds and had studied English as a foreign language in school. Participants who were educated in English-medium environments tended to talk less about language proficiency as problematic in the classroom, but still related some challenges responding to the expectations for academic language use and the high-level expectations for reading and writing. Having said that, although certain difficulties related to academic adjustment were brought up in participant interviews, my findings confirm what Andrade (2006) called L2 students' *determination* or *persistence* in overcoming academic challenges. There was strong evidence that these participants strategically positioned themselves in classroom settings to improve their chances of success and that they did not shy away from expending countless hours on their assignments for this class.

In term of cross-cultural interactions, participants were generally positive in describing their interactions with others and did not see their peers or instructor as sources of discrimination or stress. Evaluating international student experience in terms of "stress," as the literature often does, is one way of gaining perspective; however, I argue that we need more individual-level research to get a complete picture of this growing student population. The hermeneutic phenomenological research of Halic, Greenberg, and Paulus (2009); Hung and Hyun (2010); and Seo and Koro-Ljungberg (2005) uncovered a multidimensional set of findings similar to the present study, but these studies were directed at older L2 students who were entering specialized graduate-level programs. When examined against the body of existing literature on the internationalization of higher education, the present study targeted both a little-studied population (first-year undergraduates) and a little-studied context (a required mainstream FYW class) while at the same time staying true to a research tradition—hermeneutic phenomenology—that recognized the complex interplay of factors that shape L2 students' experiences in U.S. higher education.

The Arc of the Lived Experience

Links to Literature Base on FYW and L2 Writing

Next I will first link the main work of this study—perspectives on the course as participants were experiencing it—to the literature on the ubiquitous first-year writing requirement and on L2 writers in mainstream settings. This will be followed by a discussion of the arc of the participants' lived experience over time to give a view of how the journey of that semester-long course unfolded for these students.

The history of the FYW requirement in U.S. colleges in universities is long, and this course has been referred to as the one most commonly taught and taken in U.S. higher education. FYW developed more than 150 years ago with the intent of promoting students' academic literacy skill at the point of entry into the university (Beaufort, 2007; Crowley, 1998; Fleming, 2011). Research on FYW has emphasized, however, that this requirement is often conceived as a generic entity, one that focuses more on form and skill than substantive content and one whose "skills" tend not to be transferrable or applicable to the disciplinary writing situations students will face after their first year (Beaufort, 2007; Crowley, 1998; Ritter & Matsuda, 2010).

Though it would seem this requirement is as entrenched as it has always been in U.S. institutional settings, the FYW course at this university operates on a somewhat different model, offering small-group (15 students), rigorous, thematically oriented four-credit writing courses that are designed to tap into topics of intellectual and interdisciplinary interest for all students. The writing program at this university—though admittedly a relatively "elite" institutional setting—is in some ways testament to the evolution of the field of first-year writing, which draws on a new perspective about the role of content and on a different set of pedagogical tools (Fleming, 2011; Matsuda, 2012). The FYW course at the research site was meant not only to develop students' academic literacy as writers but also to be a defining experience in students' early academic career, similar to Brent's (2005) article on the growing role of first-year seminars as sites of socialization into a new academic community. In this study, it was clear from the way participants discussed this requirement that they "knew" this course would be an unavoidable part of their first year and that they entered the class with an awareness of its unique set of expectations and challenges.

It should be noted that when this university shifted from a traditional model of a two-semester Comp 101 sequence to a three-course writing requirement comprising FYW and two writing-in-the-disciplines courses, the EAP course curriculum was also modified. L2 students had previously been able to complete the required composition courses by taking a parallel series of EAP writing classes offered solely to L2 students, allowing them to fulfill the university's writing requirement in isolation from their domestic L1 peers. Through a collaborative policy decision, it was determined that students who were required to take EAP would complete a one-semester EAP course—with a Washington, DC–based theme—then follow this class with the writing course that all other first-year students were required to take. This curricular decision not only contributed to L2 students' literacy development but also promoted their inclusion in this socializing first-year writing experience. To some extent, this institutional arrangement is what motivated this study, which in turn adds to our understanding of L2 students in FYW contexts.

Because the scholarly literature of FYW tends to be more theoretical than applied—not to mention that its perspective sometimes omits L2 writers—there is a limited empirical research base in the field of FYW to engage this study's findings with. The field of L2 writing, on the other hand, is a heavily researched one, with a preponderance of research on writing expectations and the management of writing tasks or linguistic analysis of L2 texts. Such studies have a tangential relationship with the current study but may fail to present a holistic picture of how L2 students *experience* a mainstream writing course. Qualitative case studies of individual L2 writers, such as those by Leki (2007), Smoke (1994, 2004), and Spack (1997a, 2004), allowed more access to students' voices and perspectives but were often situated in classes across the mainstream curriculum—and premised on understanding individual students' responses to writing tasks and expectations more so than on other aspects of a specific classroom experience. That is not to say, however, that such studies did not bring forward valuable conclusions that both informed this research and validated its findings, notably the complex interplay of classroom factors that shape L2 students' experience as writers in the U.S. academy

(Kutz, 2004; Leki, 2007; Morita, 2004; Sternglass, 1997, 2004; Zamel, 2000; Zhou, Knoke, & Sakamoto, 2005).

The Lived Experience through Time

Building on the conclusions that L2 scholars have drawn, this study was predicated on the notion that being a part of the class is a *socio-academic* experience and that participants enter this space with certain expectations and assumptions and then negotiate interactions and tasks within that setting over time; this is consistent with the socio-academic space model this book has illustrated in Figures 1.1, 3.1, 4.1, 5.1, 6.1, 7.1, and 10.1. Interviewing participants at three points during the semester—at the beginning, the midpoint, and the end—enabled me to identify if and how participant perspectives changed as a result of time spent in the environment. As background here, it is important to emphasize that none of the participants in the study had taken a stand-alone course in writing prior to matriculating at the U.S. university, regardless of whether this was a traditional high school or university in their home country, an IB program, or even a U.S. high school exchange program. English literature courses—with expectations for writing and sometimes research—were common for participants educated in English-medium environments, but others had only experienced writing in an EFL context, and the writing they did was described as short and simple and often designed to reinforce a particular grammatical construction in English. The two participants who had transferred from universities in their home countries indicated that they had not had a writing class in high school or in college. Thus, it is clear that the notion of a stand-alone FYW class is an American construct (Berlin, 1988), one with which these L2 participants had no previous experience and little familiarity, despite their awareness of the weight of the requirement at the university. In this research context, this unfamiliarity was most certainly mitigated by their experience in the EAP academic writing class the previous semester.

Chapter 5 described participants' early entry into this world and their feeling of being simultaneously hopeful and unsure; I link this to Heidegger's philosophical notion of "thrownness"— into each new situation we are thrown from our previous socio-cultural histories and forced to respond and to make sense of the new conditions based on what we have experienced before. A key aspect of participants' rendering of their course selection process was that they wanted to mitigate stress by making a strategic selection of the course theme that would suit them best. Though they had never taken a "writing" course before, they were clearly aware of the requirement, the theme-based arrangement of the course, and its reputation for rigor. The FYW writing course is marketed as a key experience for first-year students, and even prior to arrival incoming international students are made aware of it. Participants used the tools at their disposal—peer networks, course descriptions, websites such as ratemyprofessor.com—to investigate their options and make a strategic choice. It should be noted that participants who had the most anxiety and felt the most disadvantaged in taking the class—primarily East Asian students in the case of this study— did the most homework about which section to choose. Students who had more experience in transnational settings tended to have less anxiety about managing the requirement, but still displayed a selectivity and sense of awareness when it came to their choice of course theme and, somewhat to a lesser extent, the reputation of the professor.

The strategic awareness participants displayed during the course registration process was also evident in their negotiation of the experience over time. Narrative accounts of the experience throughout the semester revealed that participants took agency to the extent that they could: In other words, they did not passively experience the course or phenomenon, but instead were self-aware members of the community who made active responses to classroom conditions.

Within the context of the classroom, participants described how actively they managed the environment and its expectations, with examples that included: speaking first in a class discussion (before anyone could share the same idea); accessing and imitating models of student writing; timing the date they signed up to lead a discussion, give a presentation, or share any classroom assignment publicly so that they could see what others had done first; and seeking external help from librarians and writing center tutors. One participant even voice-recorded a meeting with the professor in the hope of writing exactly what the professor wanted in the paper.

Findings of this study provide strong support for the conclusion that Spack (1997b, 2004) drew from her case study of a Japanese undergraduate student: students who may be perceived as passive—or even lost—are actually engaging in strategic behaviors to navigate the experience more successfully. These findings also link to Singh and Doherty's (2004) contention that L2 students are coming to the United States to seek cultural capital, and as a result—to the extent they can—they will exert agency over their learning in these classroom environments, despite the limitations they may perceive. A key goal participants articulated for studying abroad was to take advantage of an opportunity—studying at a U.S. university—in expectation of later benefits, and this is further evidenced in their accounts of the FYW experience. Throughout the semester, participants appeared to work out ways to understand the environment and maximize their chances of success. The role of agency as a characterizing feature of L2 students' experiences in writing classes is echoed in the recent work of Shapiro, Cox, Shuck, and Simnitt (2016) and has clear pedagogical implications as we strive to move beyond deficit—or difference—conceptualizations of L2 writers to "honor the knowledge and linguistic resources all students bring to our courses" (p. 32).

In the same vein, over time the words that participants used to describe the experience evolved from "uncertain" and "hopeful" to "challenging" and "meaningful," and—to some extent—from perception to reality. Though the theme was clearly a motivator in course selection, most participants began the semester unsure about what the course was really about, and there was hesitancy in their articulation of the theme. Comfort with the theme clearly grew over time for participants, and by the later interviews they were able to describe the course theme not just in practical terms but often in ways that showed how they came to "get" what the theme was all about. In other words, a change in perspective accompanied the practical knowledge they had gained. However, the significance of the course theme came to be overshadowed by the pressure of the research paper during the second half of the semester, and participants were less likely to refer to the overall course theme by the third interview. In fact, they were more likely to speak in detail about their individual topics for research and the pressure of the "big" writing assignment, generally a 12- to 15-page research paper on an individual topic related to the course theme.

Participants' reflective comments after the course ended revealed both a sense of relief and a sense of accomplishment: They constructed the experience in terms of practical gains, such as managing such a long and complex writing assignment, and in terms of the benefit of meaningful interactions with their peers and professors throughout the semester. As a researcher and as an educator, I was particularly moved by their statements of how proud they were after having finished the final research paper and how managing this complex writing task—in a foreign language no less—gave them a new confidence about conquering the challenges that were ahead. Several participants characterized it as not just a class but as an *experience*, which suggests that, at least in this regard, the institutional approach to FYW was validated. I would also argue that, while in the end participants did not feel they were *full* members of the U.S. academic discourse community, they at least felt that they inhabited a shared knowledge and discourse community as a result of living the experience. In short, they felt that they were, at least peripherally, tapped into the broader academic context of the university (Kutz, 2004; Lave & Wenger, 1991; Zuengler & Miller, 2006)—again, an important goal of the FYW course.

It is also important to add that though there was clearly a progression—or arc—in the experience that participants related, my overriding impression when listening to them was of *coherence*: Participants who began the class enthusiastically projected an enthusiastic narrative even when times got stressful, and participants who were more ambivalent about the course or the theme may have come to appreciate certain aspects of the class but remained measured about the overall experience. There was also one participant who perceived an early bias in the classroom and who retained a critical view of the class throughout the semester. Examples and descriptions that participants shared throughout the three interviews seemed to align with their original orientation to the class and also to what I would call their individual or essential character. As a researcher, this coherence across the three interviews was extremely beneficial because it gave me the sense that participants were telling their own truth as they reconstructed their experiences and that the examples and feelings that they shared were genuine and purely felt. Further, when elements of the experience were mentioned and reinforced over time by the same participant and then across participants, it made me feel I was indeed capturing the "essence" of this lived experience for this group of L2 students.

Socio-Academic Space, Interactions, and Self-Perception

From the onset, I conceived of this research in socio-academic terms—that a classroom is not just a generic space where students acquire and apply knowledge, but comprises a complex network of interactions that inform and shape the experience, in accordance with the social constructionist underpinnings of the hermeneutic phenomenological research approach and the socio-academic space model. The theoretical base that I projected would inform this study was indeed appropriate: There is no doubt that, for these participants, their sociocultural histories shaped their perspectives and responses and that meaning was created through their experiences and interactions in this socio-academic space. Vygotsky-influenced sociocultural theories of activity theory and the ZPD also applied here. Participants viewed the FYW class as an interactive experience in a specific time and place and with a particular end goal—all hallmarks of a sociocultural activity system (Donato & McCormick, 1994). Further, they often framed their interactions in this setting in relational terms and emphasized the learning that took place through mediated interactions with their professor and those they considered to be more experienced peers, supporting Vygotsky's contention that the construction of meaning is transactive and Lave and Wenger's (1991) claim that socialization into a "community of practice" is mediated through apprenticeship relationships.

This research fills a gap in the existing scholarly literature base because few studies target student experiences from a purely socio-academic perspective; instead, many examine L2 students' experience through a language or skills acquisition framework. There are clear parallels, however, between my study's findings and other scholars' work; for example, at a foundational level, it validates the work of Firth and Wagner (1997) and Swain and Deters (2007), who argued that researchers and practitioners need to look beyond the technical acquisition of language, knowledge, and skills to address how sociocultural and contextual elements and an individual's sense of identity shape experiences. The findings of this study provide strong evidence of learning as a profoundly situated social activity shaped—as L2 scholar Leki (2007) concluded—*through* relationships and interactions with others.

Relational Nature of the Experience

When participants in this study discussed themselves in the classroom environment, their construction of the experience was often relational in that they compared themselves to others in the setting based on what they perceived to be the norms and expectations for the class. When they discussed highs and lows, in other words, positive and negative experiences, almost every example linked back to an interaction with another in the classroom environment, and many highlighted instances where their work or ideas received either a positive or a negative reception.

The fact that the highs seemed to depend so much on how their contributions were received and responded to by others dovetails with Morita's (2004) contention that L2 students often struggle to be perceived as "legitimate and competent" members of the class (p. 573) and with Smoke's (1994, 2004) point that through meaningful participation in the discourse community, students can potentially move themselves from outsider to insider status.

The notion that language proficiency is often considered a technical consideration or a "stressor" in the acculturation of L2 students takes on a new dimension when considered in these terms. While it is true that participants in the study acknowledged limitations based on their perceived level of English language proficiency—or sometimes on their writing abilities—they often framed these in terms of how they "fit" in relation to others. For example, silence in the classroom often depended on whom they thought happened to know more about the topic under discussion or who could jump in fastest to express an opinion; participants felt more comfortable when other L2 students were in the class but still did not want to be perceived as the worst or near the bottom.

Even those who had high levels of English language proficiency and had been considered fluent in their home context were suddenly self-conscious about how others would perceive their abilities—how often others would "hear" their accent or notice their errors. I would argue that although on some level this could be seen as a "deficit" self-perception, it was clearly not a permanent self-view; rather, it shifted depending on the nature of the interaction or the topic under discussion. I did not conclude—as Hsieh (2007) and Fu (1995) did—that my participants internalized a deficit mentality or that they felt discriminated against or isolated from their mainstream peers. In fact, by and large their peers were seen as benign and helpful in their negotiation of this experience. Not only was the environment described as welcoming, respectful, and close-knit, but peer review and work with peer writing groups was uniformly represented as a highly positive aspect of the experience. That is not to say, however, that essentializing tendencies were absent from the sociocultural experience of my participants. It was not uncommon for participants to assume things about their American peers or even about their own cultural group. Participants mentioned the fact that Americans—sometimes called "white" or even "native" students in interviews—were better at language, reading, and writing and had cultural knowledge that they, as L2 students, lacked. This speaks to the work of scholars like Canagarajah (2002, 2006) and Norton (1997) who have emphasized that the term *native speaker* implies an ownership over the language and automatically sets L2 students in a deficit position in normative comparison to L1 peers.

Some participants even positioned people from their own linguistic or cultural background in essentializing terms, particularly some participants who called Asians "quiet" while Americans were "talkative." These same participants, however, attributed their *own* silence to other factors—implying that they were not silent by nature or culture but instead were quiet on specific occasions for their own reasons, an interesting juxtaposition of agency and self-perception with the perpetuation of stereotypical assumptions based on linguistic or cultural factors. This offers a new perspective on the source of stereotypes and essentialist assumptions—the literature seems to assume that these originate from the dominant population; in other words, that members of the U.S. university community are likely to stereotype L2 students culturally or linguistically (Kubota, 2001; Morita, 2004; Pennycook, 1994; Spack, 1997b; Zamel, 1995, 1997; Zamel & Spack, 2004). Yet the comments of these participants seemed to indicate that these assumptions work both ways and that L2 students tended to measure themselves against what they perceived to be the attributes and abilities of other students in the class.

I would add that interview comments appear to support the fact that these L2 participants were accepting of the norms and values of the dominant community and that, instead of asserting the traditions of knowledge and thinking from their home communities, they aspired to adapt to the standards of U.S. higher education and to be able to communicate "like

Americans." Though, based on my analysis of these students' context for mobility and decision to study abroad, I would argue that this was motivated by their own goals and objectives rather than a desire to fit in. Similarly, it was rare for a participant to describe a negative or discriminatory interaction with an American peer in the class, yet at the same time neither did they mention incidences where they were encouraged to share cultural or linguistic knowledge or times that they questioned or critiqued Western content or ways of knowing. And when participants mentioned an opportunity to write about topics related to their home culture, some questioned the appropriateness of this—my impression was that because the class was drawing on more American themes, they felt they had to as well. I do not mean to imply that their previous sociocultural histories were completely ignored, just that these were not brought up when participants revealed the lived experience. This seems to support Zhou, Knoke, and Sakamoto's (2005) point about L2 students assimilating into a Western knowledge framework, one that is unconsciously perpetuated by members of the dominant community, who may view L2 students as different or unfamiliar while failing to examine "the effects of reciprocal unfamiliarity" (p. 303). In other words, the L1 community perceives what it does to be normal or right and tries to help L2 students reach this level, an assimilationist point of view. Participants themselves seemed to accept this on some level, as evidenced by the adjectives they used to describe the support they got from their peers and their professor: *helpful, beneficial, kind.*

The Interplay between Course Theme and Writing

Part of my hypothesis for this study was that cultural knowledge—and its associated patterns for thinking and writing—would mediate participants' experiences since the course theme was such a key element of this FYW class. On a theoretical level, this speaks to the manner in which constructivist pedagogies—as driven by meaning making—are at play in the composition classroom, where understandings are developed based on students' interests and access to background knowledge (Kennedy, 2006). In conducting the literature review for this study, I was particularly interested in how notions of cultural knowledge and epistemology were treated in the literature. L2 scholars made mention of the role that background knowledge played in students' negotiation of academic tasks and writing assignments (Smoke, 1994, 2004; Spack, 1997a, 2004), and there has been quite a bit of emphasis on what has been called the ideological dimension of U.S. composition classrooms (Benesch, 1993, 1999; Berlin, 1988; Canagarajah, 2002; Santos, 1992, 2001). By this I mean that the content discussed in U.S. classrooms, as well as the various ways of interpreting, analyzing, and writing about it, is not ideologically neutral, though few stop to reflect on this critically.

Key insights along these lines were revealed when participants described their motivation for picking a particular theme or section of the course. Participants, in general, avoided the themes whose titles and descriptions were weighted with American cultural references. By and large, they chose themes that seemed flexible, more generic, or not as tied to a cultural knowledge base. Having said this, participants often found it a challenge to keep up with their L1 peers, whom they assumed could tap that cultural knowledge base more easily. In other words, participants in the study sometimes struggled in practical ways because they lacked a historical—or even pop culture—context for topics under discussion, and they also tended to listen more than talk in class because, to them, American students naturally knew more than they did. Further, it seemed that the L2 participants aimed to think and write in ways that were valued in the U.S. context, rather than asserting their own linguistic or cultural identities or challenging in any significant way the pedagogies and practices of the mainstream community.

A further question to consider based on the interplay between the theme and the writing is whether the course content seemed to supersede writing instruction in the class. Writing classes, both L2 and L1, have been criticized in the past for being generic, formulaic, and inapplicable to writing demands across the curriculum, and interactions with content in such classes has been called superficial and disconnected from the disciplinary domains of the institution (Crowley, 1998; Fleming, 2011; Leki, 2006). This was clearly not the case in these participants' experiences. The thematic content of the FYW course quite obviously mediated the experience, both in positive and negative ways. Expectations to engage with content went far beyond what Beaufort (2007) would call the "smorgasbord of readings" (p. 17) that most FYW students engage with. Instead, participants in this study were expected to interact in deep ways with theoretical and disciplinary perspectives on their course theme and to position their topics for writing within a scholarly literature base. This reflects calls to embed content and research more deeply in FYW curricula and at the same time it aligns with the broader trend of first-year seminar courses as a means of academic socialization and community building (Brent, 2005).

Having said that, a consequence of this scholarly thematic focus was that reading and working with sources related to the course theme was a challenging aspect of the class. Though many mentioned working with more popular sources, such as newspaper or magazine articles, on their course theme—and being more comfortable reading about and discussing them—many of these themes seemed to be situated in a critical cultural studies perspective. For participants, this meant that course content was not as straightforward as it appeared at the beginning and that the expectation for critical engagement and argumentation presented additional challenges to them throughout the semester. I would also argue that the extent to which first-year students were expected to engage content in critical and scholarly ways may well pose a challenge for even students educated and socialized in U.S. settings. Despite any challenges that may have arisen from the FYW course's level of content engagement, however, there is no doubt that this approach to classroom content moves far beyond the generic, formulaic approach that has been critiqued in the literature.

Participants further implied that their professors possessed a certain expertise related to course content, and these FYW courses drew on content in what Fleming (2011) might consider innovative, cross-disciplinary ways, but I would insert here some of Matsuda and Silva's (1999) warning that content not supersede writing instruction in FYW contexts—that is, that FYW faculty's expertise should predominantly link to writing instruction as opposed to content-area specialization. This, however, can be a challenge in the context of U.S. writing programs, which tend to draw instructors from a wide range of disciplines rather than from writing studies backgrounds.

Nevertheless, participants seemed to appreciate the depth of engagement with the course theme—provided that the theme was of interest or relevance to them. If they were ambivalent about the course theme, however, it was much more challenging for them to maintain enthusiasm for the class, though this was mitigated for some participants when they were able to select a meaningful paper topic. The importance of the course theme to the overall experience was echoed in the final interview by nearly every participant: Their advice to their peers was to choose a course theme that they were truly interested in because they will be reading, writing about, and discussing that theme for the entire semester. It's worth noting that by the third interview, participants were less likely to discuss the overall course theme and much more likely to describe their individual research paper topics and the anxiety this assignment provoked.

Writing as a Skill

The whole impetus for the FYW requirement in U.S. colleges and universities was to develop students' communicative competency as academic writers. The very nature of the requirement is testament to the value both the academic community and broader society place on this specific skill; further, it implies that writing is the most important of the communicative skills. Leki (2006) argued that this is a false perception, imposed by the "legacy" of the first-year writing requirement, and others have found that other skills, including reading, listening, and speaking, play a key role in students' academic experiences (Christison & Krahnke, 1986). While students naturally talked about writing during the interviews, there was a surprising amount of data that discussed the challenges of managing scholarly readings, leading and participating in academic discussions, and even listening comprehension in a fast-paced discussion-oriented classroom setting. Thus, it is significant to note the extent to which other skills and communicative competencies—not just writing—influenced participants' experiences. I do not believe this finding should be reduced to an L2 perspective—that these other competencies should be developed in a language classroom rather than a writing classroom. In fact, most participants, regardless of their English language proficiency, articulated these challenges, and some participants indicated that "even the American students" had a hard time reading and discussing assigned scholarly texts.

Despite seeming evidence that writing may not be the predominant skill required for successful participation in U.S. college classrooms, Zamel (1995) and Zamel and Spack (2004) found that writing was the biggest area of concern of faculty regarding L2 students in their classrooms; this suggests both that faculty continue to view L2 writers through a deficit—or at least difference—perspective and that faculty have not yet developed the awareness or tools to respond to and support diverse writers in their classrooms (Ferris, Brown, Liu, & Stine, 2011; Matsuda, Saenkhum, & Accardi, 2013). Other researchers found that students themselves are more anxious about writing than any other aspect of academic life (Berman & Cheng, 2010; Christison & Krahnke, 1986). The extent of this anxiety was evident in the experience of participants in this study, particularly as they moved into the second half of the semester, where writing expectations became more demanding. Some participants noted some ease at managing less formal tasks, such as blog posts or short reflective pieces, but the "big" writing assignments uniformly provoked anxiety.

From the interviews, it was hard to tell the extent to which participants received explicit instruction in writing. Participants indicated that were engaging with the course theme critically and that they were getting feedback on their writing and producing academic texts of varied genres, but no participant described the generic use of a textbook or any form of systematic instruction on *how* to write. That is not to say these were absent from their experiences, just that they did not come up during the interview. My impression, in fact, was that participants' writing developed as they workshopped specific aspects of their ideas and argument and that discussion of organizational structures and reasoning/support followed naturally from there. That is to say, writing instruction was more organic, driven by the needs and expectations of specific assignments rather than generic skills instruction. In addition, I noticed a growing sophistication in participants' use of the vocabulary of the field of writing studies, which demonstrated—at least in a performative sense—an awareness of the ways of thinking and critical questioning that experienced writers apply in Western classroom contexts. For example, participants used words such as "thesis," "claim," "discipline," "lens," and "analysis" and talked about being expected to demonstrate original thinking and an individual point of view. An interesting point to note is that, in engaging with these expectations and acquiring this vocabulary, these participants seemed to uncritically accept the Western cultural and epistemological preferences that underlie them (Canagarajah, 2002; Ramanathan & Atkinson, 1999). In conclusion, it would seem that the FYW experience investigated in this study indeed represented socialization into an academic discourse community in which writing skills were developed *through* interaction with content, rather than an isolated course in which students were taught generic writing forms.

10

Curricular and Pedagogical Considerations

One of the benefits of approaching this study through a framework of the internationalization of higher education was that I could think more about how big-picture trends, such as international student mobility patterns, intersected with institutional policies and practices. Obviously, a significant institutional policy is the recruitment and enrollment of international students, and U.S. colleges and universities need to understand better how these students interact with existing curricular and pedagogical approaches. This singular course is one that all undergraduate students—L1 and L2—in the university must successfully complete to fulfill a curricular requirement, which makes it an important component of the higher education curriculum. FYW provides an ideal vantage point from which to explore the lived experience of L2 students in our colleges and universities. Further, the format of the class—theme-based, small-group, discussion-oriented—and the language and academic literacy demands of the course provided more insights into the L2 experience than what might have been gained from the study of another mainstream class in another discipline.

Global Engagement within the Curriculum

Scholars have emphasized the fact that global engagement tends to be incidental to, rather than thoughtfully embedded in, our undergraduate curricula and that globally oriented courses tend to be limited to particular domains, such as foreign languages and literatures, comparative area studies, and international affairs (American Council on Education, 2012; Hayward, 2000). Thus, despite mission statements that promote global engagement, for most L1 students, content that is international or cross-cultural is unlikely to be sustained in their undergraduate education; in fact, it is most likely to be experienced on an ad hoc basis if students happen to register for a course that has a global perspective (Green, 2003; Qiang, 2003; van Gyn et al., 2009). In their chapter on cross-cultural models for writing courses, Matsuda and Silva (1999) referenced Craufurd Goodwin's point that today's graduates are "required to understand the world" and "interact with a host of people and things that are not American" (p. 246), yet for monolingual L1 students, the undergraduate curriculum at U.S. colleges and universities rarely prepares them for this in any systematic way. Writing-intensive classes, such as FYW, have immense potential to be sites for global engagement for both L1 and L2 students (Siczek & Shapiro, 2014) but are not often actively leveraged for this purpose.

At the same time, in their experience with U.S. curricula, L2 students will be more likely to engage with content, epistemology, and language that represent the perspective of the dominant (host) community. Horner and Trimbur (2002) used the term "unidirectional monolingualism" to characterize this phenomenon, and Matsuda (2006) called this the "myth of linguistic homogeneity." As long as this attitude remains in higher education circles, the adaptation for L2 students will continue to be a one-way street, which disadvantages both L1 students, who need to develop global competency, and L2 students, who have much to contribute to global and cross-cultural encounters in U.S. classrooms (Siczek, 2015; Straker, 2016; Urban & Palmer, 2014). The findings of this study suggest a similar scenario: Participants seemed to feel welcomed and broadly respected for their diversity, but they were primarily expected to engage with—and some might say assimilate to—the linguistic, content, and epistemological preferences of the U.S. academy.

As a result, although I agree that the available themes for the FYW course explore social and cultural themes that may be intellectually relevant and motivating to students, I would argue that this may not be the case for students who were not raised in U.S. society. Interviews revealed that when participants had a choice, they clearly opted for a theme they felt they had some familiarity with or one that was flexible enough that they would not be disadvantaged by the cultural knowledge that they lacked. At the same time, the literature on the internationalization of higher education—particularly on what is sometimes called internationalization-at-home—indicates that global engagement is rarely sustained across undergraduate curricula and that L1 students, despite institutional intentions for global engagement, are *not* graduating with global and cross-cultural competency (Brustein, 2007; Caruana, 2010; Hayward, 2000). Though L1 and L2 students engaged in shared tasks and activities in this FYW course, it would be hard to claim that—in any substantive way—it advanced a curriculum of global engagement.

Placement and the Multilingual Landscape

Since FYW is the "most required, most taught, and the most taken course in U.S. higher education" (Fleming, 2011, p. 1) and a formative experience in the life of any undergraduate in U.S. higher education, all institutions have to contend with the placement of all types of students into their FYW frameworks. The findings of this study offer insight into the broader debate on placement policies for L2 students.

At the research site, it had been decided that L2 students should not be segregated from L1 students when it came to the FYW requirement, although students with a TOEFL® score below a certain cutoff were required to take an EAP writing course prior to matriculation in the FYW course. As indicated earlier, all participants in this study had taken this EAP course the semester prior to the interviews. This EAP course was also thematically oriented, with course content focused on cultural perspectives within students' new city of residence: Washington, DC. Using this theme for the EAP class has proved to be both accessible and relevant for L2 students and helps prepare them for managing the theme-based environment of the FYW class. The EAP course was also designed with an understanding of writing expectations in FYW; students are expected to engage in academic research, incorporate and cite academic sources in their writing, and take a draft-based approach to producing genres common to the undergraduate curriculum in U.S. higher education, such as critical reviews of sources, annotated bibliographies, and research papers based on independently generated research questions that connect to the course theme. Because EAP courses are taught by faculty with L2 writing expertise, students can acquire academic literacy in a highly scaffolded and supported environment.

Though interview questions did not target the EAP experience, some participants drew clear comparisons between the EAP and FYW courses—for example, indicating that they were more comfortable and confident in the EAP class because everyone was "international," that the workload in EAP was more manageable, and that the professors were more focused on their support. This is in line with the general perception that sheltered English language coursework may be considered less rigorous or less "real" than mainstream courses (Vandrick, 2006) and that language proficiency and affective concerns inhibit L2 students in mainstream classroom settings (Braine, 1996; Harklau, 1994, 2000). Participants in this study revealed some similar concerns but at the same time they clearly valued sharing the FYW experience with their mainstream peers—even though it was challenging. This speaks to Matsuda and Silva (1999) and Silva's (1994, 1997) call that we approach placement for multilingual students in an "ethical" manner by placing them into appropriate learning environments. Based on my experience with this study, I do not believe that all L2 students should "sink or swim" in FYW courses, or be relegated to basic skills, developmental, or ESL-equivalent sections of the course. I would argue instead that an appropriate learning environment should include a thoughtful approach to supportive credit-bearing EAP instruction, followed by inclusion in the mainstream FYW course with well-prepared faculty—particularly in institutional settings where first-year writing is not just considered a generic skills course but a formative experience for new members of the academic community.

It was clear to me by the final interview that, although some participants would have preferred to avoid the FYW requirement, in the end all participants felt they had accomplished something meaningful through a shared experience with their L1 peers. It would appear that in this case inclusion was a worthy enterprise. However, I would emphasize that an ethical approach to placement also depends on an institutional change in perspective in alignment with the CCCC "Statement on Second Language Writing and Writers" (2009): Concern for our growing populations of culturally and linguistically diverse students cannot be left in the hands of L2 specialists teaching in isolated EAP and ESL programs. Not only does this perpetuate the notion that L2 specialists on campus are expected to "furnish all the tools" that those writers need to be academically successful (Spack, 2004, p. 36), but it also prevents the entire academic community from changing its status quo approaches to working with linguistically and culturally diverse students. The findings of this study allow institutions and educators an insider perspective on the experience of L2 students in mainstream classrooms, which supports more informed placement policies, a more critical reckoning of the multilingual landscape of U.S. higher education, and the development of new multilingual pedagogies (Hall, 2009; Matsuda, 2006, 2012; Matsuda & Silva, 1999; Matsuda et al., 2006; Silva, Leki, & Carson, 1997). To this end, part of this study's contribution comes from understanding how these L2 participants interpreted the pedagogical approaches of the FYW class.

Pedagogical Practices

Like many FYW courses, those at the research site follow a template to ensure consistency across sections regardless of the

uniqueness of the course theme or the particular approach of
the professor. Interviews revealed a number of common features
of the overall experience, including a deep interaction with a
theme; research and critical engagement with scholarly source
material; a process-oriented approach to academic writing; and
a culminating research paper 12 to 15 pages in length. Part of the
"arc" of the experience that participants revealed was that the
first half of the semester tended to consist of more topically oriented work, with lighter or more informal writing assignments,
but that the second half of the semester was strongly focused on
more individualized research and the production of an extensive
final paper. Despite these common elements, however, participants did not necessarily perceive course expectations and level
of rigor to be uniform across sections of the class. Their active
research into which class would be best—sometimes characterized as "easiest"—to register for implies that participants were
well aware of how some courses were more difficult than others.
Participants also frequently talked to peers within their network
to compare their experiences in the FYW class—and often to
determine whether they were better or worse off.

Though this study was not focused on pedagogical
approaches of the class, it was revealing to see which aspects of
teaching and learning were significant enough to be described.
Though some of these points have been referenced in previous
chapters, I believe an explicit summary of these helps illuminate
the implications of these pedagogical practices more directly and
weight their usefulness in other mainstream classroom settings.

1. Classroom Configuration

First, the size of the class and the classroom configuration clearly
influenced participants' experiences. These elements of the class
did much to make participants feel they were part of the classroom community and that they were engaged in a meaningful
learning experience. Yet participants also characterized a space
where there was a decided pressure to participate actively in
discussions and to be "on the ball" every day. In short, L2—and
most likely all—students in this class felt exposed in particular

ways; for example, performance was demanded of them, and it was difficult for them to hide or not be noticed. Sitting passively and absorbing knowledge was clearly not an option. Though this classroom configuration compared favorably to the other large, lecture-based courses participants were taking during their first year, it still required a clear level of focus and commitment.

2. The Role of Reading

The very nature of the FYW requirement implies that writing is the most important of all of the communicative skills in higher education; however, the fact that reading featured so prominently in participant descriptions of the experience was an extremely valuable finding. For some participants, concern about expectations for reading was evident as early as the course selection stage, when they wanted to avoid any course that they had heard had "heavy" reading expectations. I was also surprised at how frequently participants described academic reading assignments as stressful or burdensome during the course of the semester. While not diminishing the importance of writing in any way, this study's findings highlight the role that other skills—notably the reading and discussion of scholarly and academic texts—played in the classroom experience.

3. Peer Review

The fact that peer review was considered such a positive element of the classroom experience was also a surprising and significant outcome of this study. I had assumed that L2 students would be self-conscious or reluctant to share their work with others and intimidated by the expectation to critique the work of their peers. Indeed some participants confessed to some initial trepidation, but in the end they felt they benefitted greatly—and developed relationships they otherwise would not have—as a result of the peer review experience. I would attribute participants' receptiveness to peer review to what I have previously called their strategic response to studying in the United States: They wanted to access opportunities to be more successful in what they do so as to meet their goal.

4. The Feedback and Revision Loop

On a related note, the loop of feedback and revision was both a source of benefit and a source of stress. Participants described the feedback they received from peers and professors as helpful but sometimes overwhelming, indicating that both the instructions for the assignments and the comments from professors were sometimes challenging to interpret. They also quickly learned that the professor's response and expectations carried far more weight than the feedback of their peers. Revision was construed as an opportunity to identify weak points and improve, but some students mentioned spending countless hours in a state of confusion about what to do or how to address the comments they had received. Participants with more language anxiety were more likely to mention sentence-level errors being pointed out in their writing and that their professors tended to direct them to external sources, like the writing center, to get their grammar problems "fixed." One participant was even asked if she had taken the EAP class, implying that that class should have resolved her sentence-level writing problems, an expectation that is impossible to meet given how much is known about how long it takes to acquire fluency in a foreign language, particularly how long it takes to gain "academic" proficiency in English (Collier, 1987).

5. Role of Professor

This study asked no direct questions about participants' perception of the professor or of his/her teaching style, but most participants gave the impression of a thoughtful and inclusive instructor who was invested both in the thematic content of the course and in the success of the students. In some cases, professors acknowledged that L2 students did not have the same level of language proficiency as L1 students and that they would not grade their sentence-level writing as harshly as other students, consistent with the "ethical" perspective of some scholars such as Silva (1994, 1997). Other participants claimed their professors appeared to understand their cultural and linguistic situation but graded their work using the same standard as L1 students. A common coping strategy on the part of participants was to seek out their professor for extra help and advice, but it was clear in some cases that the professor did not feel he/she had the time or the expertise to help them enough. This would support Matsuda, Saenkhum, and Accardi's (2013) point that, though mainstream composition faculty are aware that their L2 students have unique experiences and needs, they rarely have the resources or the time to adapt their instruction enough to support them. The default advice that these participants seemed to receive was to seek their own help outside of the classroom.

The Value of a Hermeneutic Phenomenological Approach

After engaging in semi-structured conversations with my participants, getting to know them better by "hearing" their experiences through the course of the semester and analyzing the study's data and making sense of it, I have no doubt that the research approach I selected contributed meaningfully to the study. In fact, through all parts of my journey as a researcher, I kept in mind van Manen's (1990) contention that a "certain dialectic" needs to link the research questions to the method of inquiry and that these need to align with both my stake and interest in this issue as an educator. A hermeneutic phenomenological approach clearly connected to the underlying epistemological framework for this study yet at the same time situated us in the "world of lived experience" for participants who experienced this particular phenomenon (Denzin & Lincoln, 2000, p. 8). The findings of this study further reinforced the social constructionist belief that meaning is generated and shared in a social context, and the role that language and power play in shaping such experiences (Kennedy, 2006).

One of the main reasons the findings of this study validated its methodological approach was because I was able to tap into both the nature—or essence—of the lived experience for participants and to understand their interpretation of it. In particular, I believe the approach to interviewing by starting

Figure 10.1: The Socio-Academic Space Model as a Research Tool

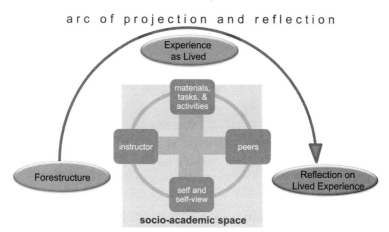

with questions about participants' sociocultural history, following with the details of the lived experience, and concluding with a reflection on the lived experience helped me access both the underlying structure (phenomenological) and the meaning participants made of the experience (hermeneutic). Applying the socio-academic space model to capture the experience over three points in time also made vivid Gadamer's notion of the forward arc of projection and the return arc of reflection, as shown in Figure 10.1.

Further, the "text" I worked with for this study, especially the audio recordings and the interview transcripts, was imbued with participants' voices, which brought forward their inner world. For me, all of these elements further committed me to what I was studying, aligned with van Manen's (1990) action-sensitive pedagogic approach to human science research.

Subjectivity, Assumptions, and Limitations

In employing this methodology, it was my responsibility to admit both my positionality and my stake in this research. Though I did see struggles in some aspects that I expected, I learned that my perspective on L2 students in an L2 writing context was necessarily limited. I would say that my own concern about their adjustment, their inclusion, in mainstream courses influenced my thinking. Because this study had an emergent design, however, I was open to the changes it might bring to my perspective; in fact, I hoped that my experience as a researcher would enlighten both my thinking and my teacher practice. Indeed, I now have new ways of understanding the FYW context that I prepare my EAP students for, as well as a deeper awareness of how resourceful and strategic L2 students can be in non-L2 settings. Interestingly, though I premised this study in some ways on the "assumptions" the rest of the higher education community imposes on culturally and linguistically diverse students, through the process of the research, I also came to question my own.

Upon the conclusion of this study, it is also important to reflect back on the study's assumptions as they related to the research approach. Listening to participants share their stories indeed reminded me that there is no "single interpretation" that constitutes the "truth" of an experience (Denzin & Lincoln, 2000; Lincoln & Guba, 2000). This phenomenon is clearly complex and multidimensional, and I found that not all participants viewed it in the same way—even those who were taking a class with the same FYW theme and professor. Further, I acknowledge that participants' experiences were shaped not just by their sociocultural histories but also by the immediate circumstance that they were facing, both in that class and in other aspects of their academic and personal lives. This meant that sometimes the interview conversations did not take the path that I had intended as a researcher, but I valued any information that participants shared because it was indeed their truth, and their experience. In the end, I should add, a meaningful structure did emerge, and I was able to capture the essence of the lived experience through these narrative accounts and in participants' own voices. Because I wanted to be very true to the language used—even though participants were interviewed in a second, or in some cases a third or fourth, language—the findings section is heavy with quoted material and not edited for standard English usage.

In terms of the study's limitations, I acknowledged early on that the relatively elite nature of the research setting, both the institution and the first-year writing program, could be conceived of as a limitation. Interview data also highlighted the fact that participants in this study likely came from positions of socioeconomic advantage and had access to more opportunity than an L2 international student in another setting. I would also add that the participants who agreed to be a part of the study—though they all met the criteria for inclusion—had a sense of responsibility and a willingness to share that may have biased my findings and conclusions. To put it another way, participating in this study was a commitment in and of itself, and those who were willing to take it on and meet with me three times during the semester may have been more likely to persist in meeting the expectations of the class. It is also possible that participants' awareness of my position at the university influenced what they said, but I did my best to encourage an equal relationship in my interactions with participants and believe they were motivated to share *because* they thought that I understood their perspective and that this research would enhance others' understanding of their experiences. This opened our channels of communication and allowed for a rich set of data.

Despite these limitations, I would argue that these findings have the potential to be meaningful across institution types, FYW settings, and even curricular and disciplinary spaces. To illustrate this point, I would like to invoke a central premise of hermeneutic phenomenological research approaches: Our goal is to connect the particular—the experience of *others* in a space we ourselves do not inhabit—to the universal, an experience that we as humans can understand regardless of whether we have directly experienced that phenomenon or not (Ricoeur, 1981). What this translates to when it comes to the final report of the study, is that the "reader belongs to the text" (van Manen, 1990, p. 180); in other words, one benefit of this research is that others can read themselves and their situations into it. Therefore, even though it is not generalizable in any quantitative sense, readers—I hope—can interpret the significance of the findings through their own frames of reference.

Recommendations

A clear objective of this study was to create more links, both between theory and practice and between policy and praxis. Based on the findings and analysis previously outlined, I'd like to put forth a series of recommendations, covering both broader research agendas and local institutional contexts.

1. Broaden the Scholarly Research Base

The first recommendation is a call for more qualitative research into the experience of transnational mobility as it relates to internationalization. Researchers need to continue moving beyond the statistics and trends to consider global mobility through new frameworks, including cosmopolitanism, language and power, English as a global language, and English language education. In terms of research at a local level, I would also advocate for more qualitative inquiry into the lived experience of linguistically and culturally diverse students in U.S. classrooms and institutions: The socio-academic space model proposed can offer a solid research tool for qualitative inquiries of this sort. We will never fully understand our policies and practices until we have a comprehensive picture of what it is like to experience them. Scholars should also broaden their agenda to other populations who are conceived of as outside the mainstream—for example, using frameworks of race, socioeconomic status, gender, and even disability studies. There is a need for an empirical body of research based on the ubiquitous FYW requirement, including comparative research on the various models for FYW instruction. It would also be extremely beneficial to study those L2 students who do not succeed in the class, and juxtapose them with the conditions under which other L2 students are more successful. Finally, I would advocate that we broaden our research base by situating more research in the mainstream curriculum, including curriculum reviews, research on faculty perspectives, and research on L2 *and* L1 perspectives, as well as cross-cultural interactions in classroom settings.

2. Tap into the Global

The second overarching recommendation relates to curricular content in the age of global engagement. It begins with a thoughtful series of questions:

- What does internationalization mean for our colleges and universities?
- How can we infuse it into our institutional practices and measure its outcomes?
- How can we tap the diversity of L2 and other multilingual students to enhance the overall global learning environment of our schools?
- What curricular spaces are most flexible in this regard?

It would appear that the first-year writing requirement will continue to be a staple of an undergraduate education in the United States and that this particular approach to FYW engages students with content—and with their peers—in deeper and more substantive ways than previous "Freshman Comp" models. Institutions and educators should explore ways to convert this interdisciplinarity and content flexibility into an opportunity to cultivate global and cross-cultural engagement. To this end, I strongly recommend that FYW programs develop course themes that are "global" in scope and intent and not primarily focused on Western or American content.

3. Question Institutional Assumptions and Arrangements

The third recommendation calls for questioning institutional assumptions and status quo arrangements in several ways:

- Reflect on our tendency to essentialize.
- Question how and why we teach and think in the ways that we do.
- Do not presume that we understand L2 students' experience and needs just because we know what country they come from or what language they speak.

In short, we should be wary of making normative comparisons and assumptions without reflectively examining our own practices and attitudes. Part of this requires a deeper consideration of the "paths" that L2 students take through U.S. higher educational systems and an examination of the various points at which they intersect with taken-for-granted policies and approaches. This should be considered part of an ethical approach to recruitment, enrollment, and ongoing support for L2 students in U.S. colleges and universities. To this end, institutions should consider opportunities to:

- build in support resources that are meaningful for *all* faculty and students, not just supports designed to assimilate L2 students into our existing socio-academic environment.
- engage L2 specialists in conversations across the university and question segregationist policies that keep both L2 students and L2 faculty out of the mainstream.
- challenge in particular the assumption that language is the domain of L2 faculty and content the domain of mainstream faculty.
- acknowledge institutional diversity of all types and integrate, or at least encourage, collaboration across units that support diverse student populations such as domestic minority students or immigrant students not classified as "international."

I strongly believe that multilingual and multicultural students are part of a new and diverse higher educational landscape and that all members of the academic community need to learn to think in new ways about the learning environments they have created—or *can* create. In addition to the obvious learning benefits, such an approach can go a long way toward "branding" our colleges and universities on the global market, retaining our streams of international students, and attracting new ones. This is particularly important as the market for international students—and even students in general—becomes increasingly competitive and subject to shifts in political and demographic circumstances.

4. Explore and Evaluate Pedagogical Practices

Fourth, in terms of teaching and learning, more work needs to be done to further awareness of the ideological dimension of both course content and pedagogy and to explore the hidden discourses that shape existing approaches. More specifically, classroom practitioners can gain insights from the content and pedagogical approaches that this study's participants found either motivating or challenging, adapt their teaching practices, and potentially pursue classroom-based action research. For example, I would recommend that educators pay particular attention to the finding that "academic literacy" is comprised of a multiplicity of skills and ways of thinking, not writing alone. We should continue to explore reading-writing links and the interaction of other skills and modes of communication. Also, the role that mediated peer interactions played in student learning—and the extent to which these shaped their overall experience in the class—is a pedagogical element that should not be neglected. Finally, because thematic content featured so prominently in participants' interpretation of the lived experience, this should be another area for deeper exploration in our FYW classrooms.

5. Consider How the FYW Course Fits
in the Broader University Context

Fifth, these research findings help situate first-year required courses like this in a larger institutional context. If it is true that "even Americans" think courses like this are extremely challenging—which should be substantiated by research—how can institutions and writing programs adjust their expectations and practices to meet the needs of first-year writers who are new to the academic discourse community? What expectations do institutions have about students' writing instruction *prior to* entering this mainstream setting? Along the same lines, this research emphasizes the importance of continuing to challenge the assumption that writing can be learned or mastered in a single writing course. Instead FYW should be conceived of as the starting point for students' journey as writers—not the be-all-end-all. At the same time, institutions should consider the role that first-year "experiences" can play in students' socio-academic socialization, particularly courses with expectations for deep engagement and a high level of interaction. This point is particularly salient for L2 students coming into U.S. colleges and universities, who may feel isolated from their mainstream peers both on campus and in classrooms. On a policy level, institutions should also assess the added value of smaller class sizes to offset the typical "huge" introductory lecture classes most first-year students take. This point is especially relevant when it is connected back to the commodification of higher education, including the recruitment and enrollment of international students, student retention, and institutional branding that helps support the school's overall positioning in the marketplace.

6. Re-Envision Classrooms as Socio-Academic Spaces

The final overarching recommendation—and the one most deeply tied to my research orientation—is that, as researchers, administrators, and educators, we remember that classrooms are sites of engagement—socio-academic spaces in which a multiplicity of actions and interactions take place. Teaching and learning is too often thought of as the transmission and application of knowledge in some generic space. As Zamel (2000) noted, however, we need to "view each classroom as a culture in its own right—a culture with its own norms, conventions, expectations—and to understand that it is the process of working within this classroom that makes it possible for participants to acquire its discourse" (p. 9). And at the same time, we need to embrace the transformative potential of interactions in our classrooms, particularly when culturally and linguistically diverse students are more and more likely to study side by side with domestic—often monolingual—students.

Conclusion

This study provided valuable insights into how L2 international students experienced and understood being part of a mainstream first-year writing course at a U.S. university, with a particular focus on how the thematic nature of the course shaped their experiences. In closing, I would like to return to where I opened: a brief narrative of an L2 international student entering the socio-academic space of the first-year writing course and examples of how she tried to make sense of this new experience. The question I posed was: How will the rest of her journey unfold?

The findings of this research study traced, in practical and deep ways, how the journey unfolded for the ten participants I interviewed during the course of the semester in which they were enrolled in the FYW course. Though this experience was sometimes punctuated by anxiety or stress, a powerful takeaway is the extent to which participants *invested* in their own opportunities. This was evident in their motivation to study in the United States, in their negotiation of the classroom experience, and in the way that they reflected upon what they had accomplished upon completion of the class. Far from being "passive" international students, these participants were often active agents of their own experiences, and their characterization of being a part of the FYW course combined a strong sense of self-awareness with a powerful understanding of others in the environment. The extent to which participants' self-perception in this setting was relational makes a strong argument for an evolved conception of classrooms as sites of engagement and interaction.

The notion of engagement takes on an even more important dimension in light of increasing institutional rhetoric on internationalization, diversity, and global engagement. Like many other universities, the research site for this study makes strong claims about the importance of promoting a student-centered learning environment that cultivates intellectual and cultural engagement, yet at the same time, participants' experience in the FYW course highlighted the dominance of American or Western cultural themes and the expectation that L2 students assimilate into the status quo academic community. It would seem that though effort was made to be inclusive and welcoming toward this diverse population of students, this institution—like many others—has still not found a way to tap this diversity as a resource or to engage domestic students on a more global level. Though intellectual engagement along the course topic was clear in most cases, neither the thematic content of the course nor the pedagogical approaches it employed seemed to advance the development of global and cross-cultural competency in any substantive way.

The findings of this study also raise questions about this specific curricular requirement and the ways it might be reconceived to better support the academic literacy needs of first-year writers and to tap into topics that are more global in their orientation. This course has been a staple of the American higher educational system for 150 years and is one of the few "required" courses for nearly every college student. The approach to FYW at the research site clearly had value: Participants were well aware of its weight, strategic in their negotiation of it, and proud of having successfully managed the experience. Nevertheless, I hope this research will give voice to students who are outside of the dominant cultural and linguistic community who inspire administrators and educators to reflect on their attitudes and practices in new and more thoughtful ways.

I also hope that readers will interpret the findings of this study through their own frames of reference and at the same time come away with a new realization that enrolling culturally and linguistically diverse students is an *opportunity*: It is not just about what they can learn from us, but what we can learn *from them* and *about ourselves* through interacting with them. By the time the final interviews were completed, each of these participants was finishing his or her first year of university in the United States. When the participants who completed follow-up interviews later reflected on the decision to study here, they unanimously agreed they had made the right decision. The insights I gained from this study were remarkable—particularly the meaningfulness of hearing participants describe their experience in their own way and in their own words. In many ways, I felt I experienced first-year writing with them. And though this particular research study ends here, more of their journey in this globally connected world is ahead.

References

Altbach, P. G. (2004). Higher education crosses borders: Can the United States remain the top destination for foreign students? *Change: The Magazine of Higher Learning, 36*(2), 18–25.

Altbach, P. G., & Knight, J. (2007). The internationalization of higher education: Motivations and realities. *Journal of Studies in International Education, 11*(3–4), 290–305.

American Council on Education. (2012). *Mapping internationalization on U.S. campuses: 2012 edition.* Retrieved from http://www.acenet. edu/newsroom/Pages/2012_Mapping-Internationalization-on-U-S–Campuses.aspx

Andrade, M. S. (2006). International students in English-speaking universities: Adjustment factors. *Journal of Research in International Education, 5*(2), 131–154.

Angelova, M., & Riazantseva, A. (1999). "If you don't tell me, how can I know?" A case study of four international students learning to write the U.S. way. *Written Communication, 16*(4), 491–525.

Atkinson, D. (2002). Toward a sociocognitive approach to second language acquisition. *The Modern Language Journal, 86*(4), 525–545.

Bartell, M. (2003). Internationalization of universities: A university culture-based framework. *Higher Education, 45*(1), 43–70.

Beaufort, A. (2007). *College writing and beyond: A new framework for university writing instruction.* Logan: Utah State University Press.

Benesch, S. (1993). ESL, ideology, and the politics of pragmatism. *TESOL Quarterly, 27*(4), 705–717.

Benesch, S. (1999). Rights analysis: Studying power relations in an academic setting. *English for Specific Purposes, 18*(4), 313–327.

Berlin, J. (1988). Rhetoric and ideology in the writing class. *College English, 50*(5), 477–494.

Berlin, J. (1992). Poststructuralism, cultural studies, and the composition classroom: Postmodern theory in practice. *Rhetoric Review, 11*(1), 16–33.

Berman, R., & Cheng, L. (2010). English academic language skills: Perceived difficulties by undergraduate and graduate students, and their academic achievement. *Canadian Journal of Applied Linguistics/Revue canadienne de linguistique appliquée, 4*(1), 25–40.

Bodycott, P. (2009). Choosing a higher education study abroad destination: What mainland Chinese parents and students rate as important. *Journal of Research in International Education, 8*(3), 349 373.

Braine, G. (1996). ESL students in first-year writing courses: ESL versus mainstream classes. *Journal of Second Language Writing, 5*(2), 91–107.

Brennan, M., & Dellow, D. A. (2013). International students as a resource for achieving comprehensive internationalization. *New Directions for Community Colleges,* (161), 27–37.

Brent, D. (2005). Reinventing WAC (again): The first-year seminar and academic literacy. *College Composition and Communication,* 253–276.

Brustein, W. I. (2007). The global campus: Challenges and opportunities for higher education in North America. *Journal of Studies in International Education, 11*(34), 382–391.

Canagarajah, A. S. (2002). Multilingual writers and the academic community: Towards a critical relationship. *Journal of English for Academic Purposes, 1*(1), 29–44.

Canagarajah, A. S. (2006). Toward a writing pedagogy of shuttling between languages: Learning from multilingual writers. *College English, 68*(6), 589–604.

Carroll, L. A. (2002). *Rehearsing new roles: How college students develop as writers.* Carbondale: Southern Illinois University Press.

Carson, J. (2001). A task analysis of reading and writing in academic contexts. In D. Belcher & A. Hirvela (Eds.), *Linking literacies: Perspectives on L2 reading-writing connections* (pp. 48–83). Ann Arbor: University of Michigan Press.

Carson, J. G., Chase, N. D., Gibson, S. U., & Hargrove, M. F. (1992). Literacy demands of the undergraduate curriculum. *Literacy Research and Instruction, 31*(4), 25–50.

Caruana, V. (2010). The relevance of the internationalised curriculum to graduate capability. In E. Jones (Ed.), *Internationalisation and the student voice: Higher education perspectives* (pp. 30–43). New York: Routledge.

Chen, C. P. (1999). Common stressors among international college students: Research and counseling implications. *Journal of College Counseling, 2*(1), 49–65.

Chen, L.H. (2008). Internationalization or international marketing? Two frameworks for understanding international students' choice of Canadian universities. *Journal of Marketing for Higher Education, 18*(1), 1–33.

Chiang, Y. M., & Schmida, M. (2006). Language identity and language ownership: Linguistic conflicts of first-year writing students. In P. Matsuda, M. Cox, J. Jordan, & C. Ortmeier Hooper (Eds.), *Second language writing in the composition classroom* (pp. 393–409). Boston: Bedford/St. Martins.

Childress, L. K. (2009). Internationalization plans for higher education institutions. *Journal of Studies in International Education, 13*(3), 289–309.

Chirkov, V., Vansteenkiste, M., Tao, R., & Lynch, M. (2007). The role of self-determined motivation and goals for study abroad in the adaptation of international students. *International Journal of Intercultural Relations, 31*(2), 199–222.

Choudaha, R., Orosz, K., & Chang, L. (2012, August). *Not all international students are the same: Understanding segments, mapping behavior.* Retrieved from www.wes.org/RAS

Chow, P. (2011). *What international students think about U.S. higher education: Attitudes and perceptions of prospective students in Africa, Asia, Europe and Latin America.* Retrieved from http://www.iie.org

Christison, M. A., & Krahnke, K. J. (1986). Student perceptions of academic language study. *TESOL Quarterly, 20*(1), 61–81.

Collier, V. P. (1987). Age and rate of acquisition of second language for academic purposes. *TESOL Quarterly, 21*(4), 617–641.

Conference on College Composition and Communication. (2009). *CCCC statement on second-language writing and writers.* Retrieved from http://www.ncte.org/cccc/resources/positions/secondlangwriting

Costino, K. A., & Hyon, S. (2007). "A class for students like me": Reconsidering relationships among identity labels, residency status, and students' preferences for mainstream or multilingual composition. *Journal of Second Language Writing, 16*(2), 63–81.

Creswell, J. (2007). *Qualitative inquiry and research design* (2nd ed.). London: Sage.

Crotty, J. M. (1998). *The foundations of social research: Meaning and perspective in the research process.* Thousand Oaks, CA: Sage.

Crowley, S. (1998). *Composition in the university: Historical and polemical essays.* Pittsburgh: University of Pittsburgh Press.

Cumming, A. (1998). Theoretical perspectives on writing. *Annual Review of Applied Linguistics, 18*(1), 61–78.

Cumming, A. (2001). Learning to write in a second language: Two decades of research. *International Journal of English Studies, 1*(2), 1–23.

De Araujo, A. A. (2011). Adjustment issues of international students enrolled in American colleges and universities: A review of the literature. *Higher Education Studies, 1*(1), 2–9.

De Wit, H. (1999). Changing rationales for the internationalization of higher education. *International Higher Education, 15*(1), 2–3.

Dean, T. (1989). Multicultural classrooms, monocultural teachers. *College Composition and Communication, 40*(1), 23–37.

Denzin, N. K., & Lincoln, Y. S. (2000). *Handbook of qualitative research.* Thousand Oaks, CA: Sage.

Dervin, F. (2011). A plea for change in research on intercultural discourses: A "liquid" approach to the study of the acculturation of Chinese students. *Journal of Multicultural Discourses, 6*(1), 37–52.

Dolby, N., & Rahman, A. (2008). Research in international education. *Review of Educational Research, 78*(3), 676–726.

Donato, R., & McCormick, D. (1994). A sociocultural perspective on language learning strategies: The role of mediation. *The Modern Language Journal, 78*(4), 453–464.

Downs, D., & Wardle, E. (2007). Teaching about writing, righting misconceptions: (Re)envisioning "First-Year Composition" as "Introduction to Writing Studies." *College Composition and Communication, 58*(4), 552–584.

Engel, L. C., & Siczek, M. (2017). A cross-national comparison of international strategies: Global citizenship and the advancement of national competitiveness. *Compare: A Journal of Comparative and International Education*, 1–19.

Englert, C. S., Mariage, T. V., & Dunsmore, K. (2006). Tenets of sociocultural theory in writing instruction research. In C.A. MacArthur, S. Graham, & J. Fitzgerald (Eds.), *Handbook of writing research* (pp. 208–221). New York: Guilford Press.

Ferris, D. (1998). Students' views of academic aural/oral skills: A comparative needs analysis. *TESOL Quarterly, 32*(2), 289–316.

Ferris, D. (2009). *Teaching college writing to diverse student populations.* Ann Arbor: University of Michigan Press.

Ferris, D., Brown, J., Liu, H. S., & Stine, M. E. A. (2011). Responding to L2 students in college writing classes: Teacher perspectives. *TESOL Quarterly, 45*(2), 207–234

Ferris, D., & Tagg, T. (1996). Academic listening/speaking tasks for ESL students: Problems, suggestions, and implications. *TESOL Quarterly, 30*(2), 297–320.

Firth, A., & Wagner, J. (1997). On discourse, communication, and (some) fundamental concepts in SLA research. *The Modern Language Journal, 81*(3), 285–300.

Fischer, K. (2011, May 29). Colleges adapt to new kinds of students from abroad. *The Chronicle of Higher Education.* Retrieved from http://chronicle.com/article/CollegesEducate-a-NewKindof/127704/

Fischer, K. (2013, October 8). US will be fastest-growing foreign-student destination, report predicts. *The Chronicle of Higher Education.* Retrieved from http://chronicle.com/article/US-Will-Be-Fastest Growing/142191/

Fleming, D. (2011). *From form to meaning.* Pittsburgh: University of Pittsburgh Press.

Fu, D. (1995). *My trouble is my English: Asian students and the American dream.* Portsmouth, NH: Boynton/Cook.

Ginther, A., & Grant, L. (1996). *A review of the academic needs of native English speaking college students in the United States.* Princeton, NJ: Educational Testing Service.

Green, M. F. (2003, January). The challenge of internationalizing undergraduate education: Global learning for all. *Proceedings of the Global Challenges and US Higher Education Conference.* Retrieved from http://ducis.jhfc.duke.edu/archives/globalchallenges/pdf/green.pdf

Halic, O., Greenberg, K., & Paulus, T. (2009). Language and academic identity: A study of the experiences of non-native English speaking international students. *International Education, 38*(2), 73–93.

Hall, J. (2009). WAC/WID in the next America: Redefining professional identity in the age of the multilingual majority. *The WAC Journal, 20,* 33–49.

Hall, J. (2014). Multilinguality is the mainstream. In B. Horner & K. Kopelson (Eds.), *Reworking English in rhetoric and composition: Global interrogations, local interventions* (pp. 31–48). Carbondale: Southern Illinois University Press.

Harklau, L. (1994). ESL versus mainstream classes: Contrasting L2 learning environments. *TESOL Quarterly, 28*(2), 241–272.

Harklau, L. (2000). From the "good kids" to the "worst": Representations of English language learners across educational settings. *TESOL Quarterly, 34*(1), 35–67.

Hayward, F. M. (2000). *Internationalization of US higher education. Preliminary status report, 2000.* Washington, DC: American Council on Education.

Heng, T. T. (2016). Different is not deficient: Contradicting stereotypes of Chinese international students in US higher education. *Studies in Higher Education,* 1–15.

Hinkel, E. (1999). *Culture in second language teaching and learning.* Cambridge, England: Cambridge University Press.

Hinkel, E. (2002). *Second language writers' text: Linguistic and rhetorical features.* Mahwah, NJ: Lawrence Erlbaum.

Hinkel, E. (Ed.). (2005). *Handbook of research in second language teaching and learning.* Mahwah, NJ: Lawrence Erlbaum.

Hofstede, G. (1980). Motivation, leadership, and organization: Do American theories apply abroad? *Organizational dynamics, 9*(1), 42–63.

Horner, B. (2006). Introduction: Cross-language relations in composition. *College English, 68*(6), 569–573.

Horner, B., & Trimbur, J. (2002). English only and US college composition. *College Composition and Communication, 53*(4), 594–630.

Hsieh, M. H. (2007). Challenges for international students in higher education: One student's narrated story of invisibility and struggle. *College Student Journal, 41*(2), 379–391.

Huang, L. S. (2010). Seeing eye to eye? The academic writing needs of graduate and undergraduate students from students' and instructors' perspectives. *Language Teaching Research, 14*(4), 517–539.

Hung, H. L., & Hyun, E. (2010). East Asian international graduate students' epistemological experiences in an American university. *International Journal of Intercultural Relations, 34*(4), 340–353.

Hunter, B., White, G. P., & Godbey, G. C. (2006). What does it mean to be globally competent? *Journal of Studies in International Education, 10*(3), 267–285.

Ibrahim, N., & Penfield, S. (2005). Dynamic diversity: New dimensions in mixed composition classes. *ELT Journal, 59*(3), 217–225.

ICEF. (2014). *Summing up international student mobility in 2014*. Retrieved from http://monitor.icef.com/2014/02/summing-up-international-student-mobility-in 2014/

Institute of International Education. (2013). *International student totals by place of origin, 2011/12–2012/13*. Retrieved from http://www.iie.org/opendoors

Institute of International Education. (2016). *Open Doors data*. Retrieved from http://www.iie.org/opendoors

Jones, E., & Killick, D. (2007). Internationalisation of the curriculum. In E. Jones & S. Brown (Eds.), *Internationalising higher education* (pp. 109–119). London: Routledge.

Kell, P., & Vogl, G. (2008). Perspectives on mobility, migration and well-being of international students in the Asia Pacific. *International Journal of Asia-Pacific Studies, 4*(1), 21–31.

Kennedy, M. L. (Ed.). (2006). *Theorizing composition: A critical sourcebook of theory and scholarship in contemporary composition studies*. Greenwich, CT: Information Age Publishing.

Knight, J. (2004). Internationalization remodeled: Definition, approaches, and rationales. *Journal of Studies in International Education, 8*(1), 5–31.

Kozulin, A., Gindis, B., Ageyev, V., & Miller, S. (Eds.). (2003). *Vygotsky's educational theory in cultural context*. Cambridge, England: Cambridge University Press.

Kreber, C. (2009). Different perspectives on internationalization in higher education. *New Directions for Teaching and Learning, 2009*(118), 1–14.

Kubota, R. (2001). Discursive construction of the images of US classrooms. *TESOL Quarterly, 35*(1), 9–38.

Kutz, E. (2004). From outsider to insider: Studying academic discourse communities across the curriculum. In V. Zamel, & R. Spack (Eds.), *Crossing the curriculum: Multilingual learners in college classrooms* (pp. 76–93). Mahwah, NJ: Lawrence Erlbaum.

Lantolf, J. P., & Pavlenko, A. (1995). Sociocultural theory and second language acquisition. *Annual Review of Applied Linguistics, 15*(1), 108–124.

Lantolf, J. P., & Poehner, M. E. (Eds.). (2008). *Sociocultural theory and the teaching of second languages*. London: Equinox.

Lave, J., & Wenger, E. (1991). *Situated learning: Legitimate peripheral participation*. Cambridge, England: Cambridge University Press.

Laverty, S. M. (2003). Hermeneutic phenomenology and phenomenology: A comparison of historical and methodological considerations. *International Journal of Qualitative Methods, 2*(3), 21–35.

Leask, B. (2001). Bridging the gap: Internationalizing university curricula. *Journal of Studies in International Education, 5*(2), 100–115.

Lee, J. J. (2008). Beyond borders: International student pathways to the United States. *Journal of Studies in International Education, 12*(3), 308–327.

Lee, J. J., & Rice, C. (2007). Welcome to America? International student perceptions of discrimination. *Higher Education, 53*(3), 381–409.

Leki, I. (1995). Coping strategies of ESL students in writing tasks across the curriculum. *TESOL Quarterly, 29*(2), 235–260.

Leki, I. (2006). The legacy of first-year composition. In P. K Matsuda, C. Ortmeier Hooper, & X. You (Eds.), *The Politics of second language writing: In search of the promised land* (pp. 59–74). West Lafayette, IN: Parlor Press.

Leki, I. (2007). *Undergraduates in a second language: Challenges and complexities of academic literacy development*. Mahwah, NJ: Lawrence Erlbaum.

Leki, I., & Carson, J. (1994). Students' perceptions of EAP writing instruction and writing needs across the disciplines. *TESOL Quarterly, 28*(1), 81–101.

Leki, I., & Carson, J. (1997). "Completely different worlds": EAP and the writing experiences of ESL students in university courses. *TESOL Quarterly, 31*(1), 39–69.

Leki, I., Cumming, A., & Silva, T. (2008). *A synthesis of research on second language writing in English*. New York: Routledge.

Lewthwaite, M. (1996). A study of international students' perspectives on cross cultural adaptation. *International Journal for the Advancement of Counselling, 19*(2), 167–185.

Lincoln, Y. S., & Guba, E. G. (2000). Paradigmatic controversies, contradictions, and emerging confluences. In Y. S. Lincoln & N. K. Denzin (Eds.), *The handbook of qualitative research* (pp. 97–128). Thousand Oaks, CA: Sage.

Lobnibe, J. F. (2009). International students and the politics of difference in US higher education. *Journal for Critical Education Policy Studies, 7*(2), 346–368.

MacArthur, C. A., Graham, S., & Fitzgerald, J. (Eds.). (2006). *Handbook of writing research.* New York: Guilford Press.

McCaffrey, G., Raffin-Bouchal, S., & Moules, N. J. (2012). Hermeneutics as research approach: A reappraisal. *International Journal of Qualitative Methods, 11*(3), 214–229.

McKay, S. L. (1993). Examining L2 composition ideology: A look at literacy education. *Journal of Second Language Writing, 2*(1), 65–81.

Martin-Jones, M., & Heller, M. (1996). Introduction to the special issues on education in multilingual settings: Discourse, identities, and power: Part I: Constructing legitimacy. *Linguistics and Education, 8*(1), 3–16.

Matsuda, P. K. (2006). The myth of linguistic homogeneity in US college composition. *College English, 68*(6), 637–651.

Matsuda, P.K. (2012). Teaching composition in the multilingual world: Second language writing in composition studies. In K. Ritter & P. K. Matsuda (Eds.), *Exploring Composition Studies* (pp. 36–51). Logan: Utah State University Press.

Matsuda, P., Cox, M., Jordan, J., & Ortmeier-Hooper, C. (Eds.). (2006). *Second language writing in the composition classroom.* Boston: Bedford/St. Martins.

Matsuda, P. K., Saenkhum, T., & Accardi, S. (2013). Writing teachers' perceptions of the presence and needs of second language writers: An institutional case study. *Journal of Second Language Writing, 22*(1), 68–86.

Matsuda, P. K., & Silva, T. (1999). Cross-cultural composition: Mediated integration of US and international students. *Composition Studies, 27*(1), 15–30.

Mazzarol, T., & Soutar, G. N. (2002). "Push-pull" factors influencing international student destination choice. *International Journal of Educational Management, 16*(2), 82–90.

Merriam, S. (2009). *Qualitative research: A guide to design and implementation.* San Francisco: Jossey-Bass.

Misra, R., Crist, M., & Burant, C. J. (2003). Relationships among life stress, social support, academic stressors, and reactions to stressors of international students in the United States. *International Journal of Stress Management, 10*(2), 132–148.

Mori, S. (2000). Addressing the mental health concerns of international students. *Journal of Counseling and Development, 78,* 137–144.

Morita, N. (2004). Negotiating participation and identity in second language academic communities. *TESOL Quarterly, 38*(4), 573–603.

NAFSA. (2016). *International education data & statistics*. Retrieved from http://www.nafsa.org

Nakkula, M., & Ravitch, S. (1998). *Matters of interpretation: Reciprocal transformation in therapeutic and developmental relationships with youth*. San Francisco: Jossey Bass.

Nelson, G., & Carson, J. (2006). Cultural issues in peer response: Revisiting "culture." In K. Hyland & F. Hyland (Eds.), *Feedback in second language writing: Contexts and issues* (pp. 42–59). New York: Cambridge University Press.

Norton, B. (1997). Language, identity, and the ownership of English. *TESOL Quarterly, 31*(3), 409–429.

Ortmeier-Hooper, C. (2008). "English may be my second language, but I'm not ESL." *College Composition and Communication, 59*(3), 389–419.

Paltridge, B., Starfield, S., & Tardy, C. M. (2016). *Ethnographic perspectives on academic writing*. Oxford, England: Oxford University Press.

Patton, M. Q. (2002). *Qualitative research and education methods*. Thousand Oaks, CA: Sage.

Pennycook, A. (1994). *The cultural politics of English as an international language*. London: Longman.

Prior, P. (2006). A sociocultural theory of writing. In C.A. MacArthur, S. Graham, & J. Fitzgerald (Eds.), *Handbook of writing research*, (pp. 54–66). New York: Guilford Press.

Qiang, Z. (2003). Internationalization of higher education: Towards a conceptual framework. *Policy Futures in Education, 1*(2), 248–270.

Raimes, A. (1987). Language proficiency, writing ability, and composing strategies: A study of ESL college student writers. *Language Learning, 37*(3), 439–468.

Raimes, A. (1991). Out of the woods: Emerging traditions in the teaching of writing. *TESOL Quarterly, 25*(3), 407–430.

Ramanathan, V., & Atkinson, D. (1999). Individualism, academic writing, and ESL writers. *Journal of Second Language Writing, 8*(1), 45–75.

Ricoeur, P. (1981). *Hermeneutics and the human sciences: Essays on language, action and interpretation*. Cambridge, England: Cambridge University Press.

Ritter, K., & Matsuda, P. K. (2010). *Exploring composition studies: Sites, issues, perspectives*. Boulder: University Press of Colorado.

Rizvi, F. (2005). Identity, culture and cosmopolitan futures. *Higher Education Policy, 18*(4), 331–339.

Santos, T. (1992). Ideology in composition: L1 and ESL. *Journal of Second Language Writing, 1*(1), 1–15.

Santos, T. (2001). The place of politics in second language writing. In T. Silva & P. K. Matsuda (Eds.), *On second language writing* (pp. 173–190). Mahwah, NJ: Lawrence Erlbaum.

Schwandt, T. A. (2000). Three epistemological stances for qualitative inquiry. In N. K. Denzin & Y.S. Lincoln (Eds.), *Handbook of qualitative research.* Thousand Oaks, CA: Sage.

Seidman, I. (1998). *Interviewing as qualitative research: A guide for researchers in education and the social sciences.* New York: Teachers College Press.

Seo, S., & Koro-Ljungberg, M. (2005). A hermeneutical study of older Korean graduate students' experiences in American higher education: From Confucianism to western educational values. *Journal of Studies in International Education, 9*(2), 164–187.

Shapiro, S., Cox, M., Shuck, G., & Simnitt, E. (2016). Teaching for agency: From appreciating linguistic diversity to empowering student writers. *Composition Studies, 44*(1), 31–52.

Siczek, M. (2015). Developing global competency in US higher education: Contributions of international students. *CATESOL Journal, 27*(2), 5–21.

Siczek, M., & Shapiro, S. (2014). Developing writing-intensive courses for a globalized curriculum through WAC-TESOL collaborations. In T. Myers Zawacki & M. Cox (Eds.), *WAC and second language writers: Research towards linguistically and culturally inclusive programs and practices* (pp. 329–346). Anderson, SC: Parlor Press.

Silva, T. (1993). Toward an understanding of the distinct nature of L2 writing: The ESL research and its implications. *TESOL Quarterly, 27*(4), 657–677.

Silva, T. (1994). An examination of writing program administrators' options for the placement for ESL students in their first year writing classes. *Writing Program Administration, 18*(1/2), 37–43.

Silva, T. (1997). On the ethical treatment of ESL writers. *TESOL Quarterly, 31*(2), 359–363.

Silva, T., Leki, I., & Carson, J. (1997). Broadening the perspective of mainstream composition studies: Some thoughts from the disciplinary margins. *Written Communication, 14*(3), 398–428.

Singh, P., & Doherty, C. (2004). Global cultural flows and pedagogic dilemmas: Teaching in the global university contact zone. *TESOL Quarterly, 38*(1), 9–42.

Singh, P., & Thuraisingam, T. (2007). A hermeneutic phenomenological approach to socio cultural and academic adjustment experiences of international students. *18th ISANA International Education Association Conference Proceedings*. Retrieved from http://proceedings.com.au/isana/docs/2007/Paper_Singh.pdf

Smith, R. A., & Khawaja, N. G. (2011). A review of the acculturation experiences of international students. *International Journal of Intercultural Relations, 35*(6), 699–713.

Smoke, T. (1994). Writing as a means of learning. *College ESL, 4*(2), 1–11.

Smoke, T. (2004). Lessons from Ming: Helping students use writing to learn. In V. Zamel & R. Spack (Eds.), *Crossing the curriculum: Multilingual learners in college classrooms* (pp. 61–74). Mahwah, NJ: Lawrence Erlbaum.

Spack, R. (1997a). The acquisition of academic literacy in a second language: A longitudinal case study. *Written Communication, 14*(1), 3–62.

Spack, R. (1997b). The rhetorical construction of multilingual students. *TESOL Quarterly, 31*(4), 765–774.

Spack, R. (2004). The acquisition of academic literacy in a second language: A longitudinal case study, updated. In V. Zamel & R. Spack (Eds.), *Crossing the curriculum: Multilingual learners in college classrooms* (pp. 19–45). Mahwah, NJ: Lawrence Erlbaum.

Sternglass, M. S. (1997). *Time to know them: A longitudinal study of writing and learning at the college level.* Mahwah, NJ: Lawrence Erlbaum.

Sternglass, M. S. (2004). "It became easier over time": A case study of the relationship between writing, learning, and the creation of knowledge. In V. Zamel & R. Spack (Eds.), *Crossing the curriculum: Multilingual learners in college classrooms* (pp. 47–59). Mahwah, NJ: Lawrence Erlbaum.

Straker, J. (2016). International student participation in higher education: Changing the focus from "international students" to "participation." *Journal of Studies in International Education, 20*(4), 299–318.

Stromquist, N. P. (2007). Internationalization as a response to globalization: Radical shifts in environments. *Higher Education,* *53*(1), 81–105.

Swain, M., & Deters, P. (2007). "New" mainstream SLA theory: Expanded and enriched. *The Modern Language Journal, 91*(s1), 820–836.

Taylor, J. (2004). Toward a strategy for internationalisation: Lessons and practice from four universities. *Journal of Studies in International Education, 8*(2), 149–171.

Thomason, A. (2013, October 15). Diversity aside, international students bring a financial incentive. *The Chronicle of Higher Education.* Retrieved from http://chronicle.com/blogs/bottomline/diversity-aside-international-students bring-a-financial-incentive/

Urban, E. L., & Palmer, L. B. (2014). International students as a resource for internationalization of higher education. *Journal of Studies in International Education, 18*(4), 305–324.

Van der Wende, M. (1999). An innovation perspective on internationalization of higher education institutionalisation: The critical phase. *Journal of Studies in International Education, 3*(1), 3–14.

Van der Wende, M. C. (2001). Internationalisation policies: About new trends and contrasting paradigms. *Higher Education Policy, 14*(3), 249–259.

Van Gyn, G., Schuerholz-Lehr, S., Caws, C., & Preece, A. (2009). Education for world mindedness: Beyond superficial notions of internationalization. *New Directions for Teaching and Learning,* (118), 25–38.

Van Manen, M. (1990). *Researching lived experience: Human science for an action sensitive pedagogy.* Albany: SUNY Press.

Vandrick, S. (2006). Shifting sites, shifting identities: A thirty-year perspective. In P. K. Matsuda, C. Ortmeier-Hooper, & X. You (Eds.), *Politics of second language writing* (pp. 280–293). West Lafayette, IN: Parlor Press.

Villamil, O. S., & de Guerrero, M. C. M. (2006). Sociocultural theory: A framework for understanding the social-cognitive dimensions of peer feedback. In K. Hyland & F. Hyland (Eds.), *Feedback in second language writing: Contexts and issues* (pp. 23–41). New York: Cambridge University Press.

Wadsworth, B. C., Hecht, M. L., & Jung, E. (2008). The role of identity gaps, discrimination, and acculturation in international students' educational satisfaction in American classrooms. *Communication Education, 57*(1), 64–87.

Ward, C., & Searle, W. (1991). The impact of value discrepancies and cultural identity on psychological and sociocultural adjustment of sojourners. *International Journal of Intercultural Relations, 15*(2), 209–224.

Watson-Gegeo, K. A. (2004). Mind, language, and epistemology: Toward a language socialization paradigm for SLA. *The Modern Language Journal, 88*(3), 331–350.

Wiersma, W., & Jurs, S. G. (2005). *Research methods in education* (8th ed.). Boston: Allyn and Bacon.

Yeh, C. J., & Inose, M. (2003). International students' reported English fluency, social support satisfaction, and social connectedness as predictors of acculturative stress. *Counselling Psychology Quarterly, 16*(1), 15–28.

Zamel, V. (1995). Strangers in academia: The experiences of faculty and ESL students across the curriculum. *College Composition and Communication, 46*(4), 506–521.

Zamel, V. (1997). Toward a model of transculturation. *TESOL Quarterly, 31*(2), 341–352.

Zamel, V. (2000). Engaging students in writing-to-learn: Promoting language and literacy across the curriculum. *Journal of Basic Writing, 19*(2), 3–21.

Zamel, V., & Spack, R. (Eds.). (2004). *Crossing the curriculum: Multilingual learners in college classrooms*. Mahwah, NJ: Lawrence Erlbaum.

Zhou, R., Knoke, D., & Sakamoto, I. (2005). Rethinking silence in the classroom: Chinese students' experiences of sharing indigenous knowledge. *International Journal of Inclusive Education, 9*(3), 287–311.

Zuengler, J., & Miller, E. R. (2006). Cognitive and sociocultural perspectives: Two parallel SLA worlds? *TESOL Quarterly, 40*(1), 35–58.

Index

academic literacy: demands in writing curriculum, 10–11, 149, 163, 183; in participant FYW experience, 163, 180. *See also* class discussion; reading; vocabulary; writing

action sensitive pedagogic approach, xv, 60, 61, 174

activity theory, 19, 62–63, 155–156

agency, 15, 152–153, 158, 182. *See also* strategic awareness

Berlin, J., 12, 13, 151, 160

Canagarajah, S., 9, 141, 158, 160, 180

class discussion, participants: comparison of L1 vs. L2 peers in, 82–84, 97–99, 103, 157–158; expectation for participation in, 81, 97–99, 107, 170–171; follow-up interviews on experience with, 122–123, 128, 135; listening comprehension and, 84, 163; oral English proficiency and, 84, 86, 98–99, 103; pace of, 84, 97–99, 107, 163; perceived benefits of, 81, 92, 98, 107; reception to ideas in, 100–101; silence in, 103, 158

classroom culture, 15, 63, 151, 180–182. *See also* socio-academic relationships; socio-academic space

co-curricular experiences, participants: fraternities and sororities, 120, 121, 132; internship experience, 125–126, 128, 132; off-campus living, 126, 132; study abroad, 120

constructivism, 55, 62, 159

content knowledge: in participants' classroom experience, 82–83, 92– 93, 111, 146, 159, 160; Western epistemological and content knowledge base, 14, 17–18, 146, 159, 160, 164, 183. *See also* first-year writing; first-year writing course theme

cosmopolitanism, 16, 140–141, 145, 177

cultural and linguistic diversity: deficit perception of, xv, 7, 8–9, 17, 158, 163 (*see also* institutional context); as a resource for global engagement, 14, 16, 17, 166, 178, 182–183; of study participants, 38–40, 140–141; on U.S. college campuses, 144–145.